PRAISE

Midlife Medium: A Genealogist's Quest to Converse with the Dead

"Sharon DeBartolo Carmack's *Midlife Medium: A Genealogist's Quest to Converse with the Dead* is written with honesty, wisdom, and the awareness that essential questions of life after death still confound so many of us. Carmack is a gifted storyteller, and her engaging, spirited journey comes to us with both humor and serious intent. A clear guide for anyone with questions, and anyone open to unanticipated answers." — **Dinty W. Moore, author of *To Hell With It* and *The Accidental Buddhist***

"Carmack's keen writing endearingly portrays her family throughout her journey, from her obliging partner to her grown daughter, Laurie, who's consistently wary of Mom's mediumship. Its depiction of family relationships shines." —***Kirkus Reviews***

"*Midlife Medium: A Genealogist's Quest to Converse with the Dead* is an intriguing and remarkable book. With honesty, insight, and humor, Sharon DeBartolo Carmack, one of America's most skilled and respected family historians and authors, takes us along on her fascinating journey. She explores the possibilities that we all *do* survive on 'The Other Side,' and our loved ones are eager to contact us and ready to help us. Like every good genealogist, she carefully weighs the evidence pro and con as she builds her case to substantiate her conclusions. This book tested my brain and warmed my heart: it's a loving reinforcement that indeed we are all spiritual beings seeking a human experience—and are truly *one*." —**Henry Z Jones, author of *Psychic Roots: Serendipity and Intuition in Genealogy* and *More Psychic Roots: Further Adventures in Serendipity and Intuition in Genealogy***

"A five-star read! Sharon's journey to become a medium in her fifties is both humorous and profound. Written in a conversational voice, it feels as if Sharon is sitting next to you over a cup of tea and sharing her victories and calamities. *Midlife Medium* is funny because it's so amazingly honest."—**Sandra Champlain, author of *We Don't Die: A Skeptic's Discovery of Life After Death* and radio show host of We Don't Die Radio and Shades of the Afterlife**

"Many religions have a concept of some state beyond this physical life. Spiritualism is different because it does not demand that you have faith or believe. Rather, it provides evidence that life continues beyond the change we call death. This evidence is delivered through the gift of mediumship. Sharon has written this book that records her journey of experience toward becoming a medium. Mediumship is not a career choice, but rather a vocation through which you can touch lives. It brings about a wonderful transformation, which can change lives for the better, dispel grief, and ultimately serve humanity. Sharon's experience makes fascinating reading and is well crafted to provide the reader with a personal insight into a world that may appear strange to some people. But through that world, and the mediumship experience, remarkable things are possible, and lives can and are transformed forever." —**Minister David R. Bruton, president of the Spiritualists' National Union, principal of Arthur Findlay College**

"Anyone who's ever explored their family history wishes they could communicate with their ancestors, and finally, there's a book for that! In *Midlife Medium*, renowned genealogist Sharon DeBartolo Carmack—with her trademark humor, grit, and candor on full display—invites us to peek over her shoulder on her fascinating journey into Spiritualism and becoming a credentialed medium. This book is your ticket to join her pioneering quest!"—**Megan Smolenyak, author of *In Search of Our Ancestors: 101 Inspiring Stories of Serendipity and Connection***

"If you have always wondered how mediumship works and whether it is really possible to communicate with the dead, this book is the key to unlocking the mystery. Sharon DeBartolo Carmack weaves a captivating story as she strives to comprehend her lifetime of spiritual unfoldment, from schoolgirl spell caster to fully qualified medium. As a professional genealogist, highly skilled at unearthing old documents and piecing together the lives of our ancestors, Carmack takes a meticulous approach, researching the history, science, and philosophy of mediumship and examining the evidence from every scientific and spiritual angle. In her new book, *Midlife Medium*, she has created a must-read guide full of riveting information and facts for anyone interested in learning more about mediumship, all written with her unique satirical sense of humor, which will keep you turning the pages. I highly recommend this book, which I'm sure will inspire and support you in your own quest to find your truth."—**Ann Théato, psychic medium, tutor, host and founder of the Psychic Matters! podcast**

"Frank, lighthearted, and good fun to read, *Midlife Medium* demystifies afterlife communication. Sharon Carmack's mediumship quest shows how healing relationships between the living and dead is both possible and enchanting."—**Melanie Alberts, psychic artist and host of *Psychic Playdate* podcast**

"Genealogists worth their salt have long used Sharon DeBartolo Carmack's helpful guidebooks to find their ancestors and tell their stories. Now, in this flowing and unexpectedly funny memoir, she delivers evidence of how our departed loved ones survive in spirit, keen to communicate and reconnect. Just follow Sharon's lead and you will sense them too." —**Joseph Ditta, archivist and author of *Then & Now: Gravesend, Brooklyn***

"*Midlife Medium* is the inspiring and informative story of Sharon Carmack's journey from skeptic to practicing medium. Sharon writes with a clear eye and wry humor of her many experiences as an aspiring medium. Her book also contains useful information about the history of Spiritualism and practical exercises for mediumship development. If you have ever wondered what it's really like to become a medium, this book is a must read."—**Carolyn Marie Wilkins, psychic medium and author of *Death at a Seance: A Carrie McFarland Psychic Mystery***

"I have never read a more accurate description of the path from genealogist to Spiritualist than *Midlife Medium*. Sharon authentically captures the doubts and experiences that led her to work with the ancestors through mediumship. I've trod many of the same paths and can wholeheartedly recommend this journey."—**Nancy Hendrickson, author of *Ancestral Tarot* and *Unofficial Guide to Ancestry.com***

"In this lively and arresting memoir, Sharon DeBartolo Carmack, a career genealogist skilled in uncovering stories of the dead, becomes our spirit guide into worlds that most will never enter. *Midlife Medium: A Genealogist's Quest to Converse with the Dead* is both a journey of the head—from skepticism to fully immersed practice in Spiritualism—and a journey of the heart, a story of forgiveness and healing between mothers and daughters. Just as a medium mediates between the spirit world and the land of the living, Carmack artfully mediates between her story and ours. And we, her lucky readers, are changed by the encounter." —**Rebecca McClanahan, author of *The Tribal Knot: A Memoir of Family, Community, and a Century of Change* and *Word Painting: A Guide to Writing More Descriptively***

Midlife Medium:
A Genealogist's Quest to Converse with the Dead

by Sharon DeBartolo Carmack

ISBN 978-1-64663-706-5

REVIEW COPY: This is an advanced printing subject to corrections and revisions.

Published by

köehlerbooks™

3705 Shore Drive
Virginia Beach, VA 23455
800-435-4811
www.koehlerbooks.com

Midlife
MEDIUM

*A Genealogist's Quest to
Converse with the Dead*

Sharon DeBartolo Carmack

VIRGINIA BEACH
CAPE CHARLES

For Laurie, who helped make my journey more interesting.

Table of Contents

Note to the Reader

For the most part, I have changed or omitted some people's names to protect their privacy, and I have also modified or changed identifying features. My daughter, Laurie, loves seeing her name in print, so I've used her name. My partner asked that I change his name, so instead of "Sweetheart," I'm using his real name, Jim.

Prologue

I was destined to die at age fifty-six.

My stepmother, Linda, sat across from me, the sepia-toned Ouija board between us on a TV tray. Our fingertips rested lightly on the plastic indicator. Her nails were always neatly manicured with an orangey-red polish. She wore a diamond cocktail ring on her right hand, and a two-carat diamond solitaire with diamond ring guard on her wedding finger. The stones glittered from the ceiling light. I wore my usual bell-bottomed jeans, a tight T-shirt, and a necklace with the word *Witch* around my neck. Linda was just ten years older than I. She didn't mind my goth-witchy phase and didn't hesitate when I asked her to do the Ouija board with me.

"Is anyone there?" she asked of the board. We both stared at it. Within seconds, the planchette moved around the board in a circular motion, then it pointed to YES.

"You're moving it," I accused her. I didn't trust Linda. She had only recently married my father and was still trying to get in my good graces. She knew my father and I were close.

"No, I'm not!"

I don't recall all the questions we asked, but some things I'll never forget. The spirit gave his name as Pontius. I looked at Linda. "As in

Pontius Pilate?" She shrugged. Whether we asked for confirmation, I don't remember.

The one question I know I asked was, "When will I die?" What possessed me to ask this, I have no idea.

The planchette moved quickly and pointed first to the numeral *5*, then to the numeral *6*.

Okay. So, I'm going to die at age fifty-six. That was a long way off, and besides, who takes that kind of thing seriously when you're seventeen?

Shortly after that fateful, fall, fifty-sixth birthday in 2012, I fell into a funk I couldn't shake. I moped the day away, going through the motions of my routine without passion or enthusiasm for anything. Like an old Polaroid instant photograph, my colors were no longer brilliant but washed out, faded to unnatural hues. Then the dormant memory of what the Ouija board predicted came back to me.

I'd lived an eventful life with regular high points that kept my inner self buoyant. I'd had a successful career as a high-profile professional genealogist, writer, and public speaker. I'd returned to school for a master's degree a month after I turned fifty-three and graduated with distinction. I started a second career as a college adjunct faculty, teaching graduate creative nonfiction writing. Some of my literary essays had been published. I'd raised a charismatic, intelligent, and responsible daughter and had become a grandmother. I'd wrapped up one marriage and began another. (It's true: "Love is lovelier the second time around.") Yet my spirit had dematerialized. I felt like a has-been, a once-favorite T-shirt now forgotten at the bottom of a dresser drawer. I told my thirty-year-old daughter, Laurie, with a sigh as mournful as those heard round the world when the news broke that Hostess went out of business, "I don't feel I have anything to live for."

When you turn fifty-six, have probably absorbed too much hair dye in your brain, are stuck in a funk, and realize that the odds of living another fifty-six years are slim, the Ouija board's prediction takes on new meaning. The future held no highs, no Twinkies, on the horizon. I had once wanted to live to be one hundred so I could see a photo of my drooping, wrinkled face and dentured smile on a raspberry-red Smucker's label on the *Today Show*, the old folks' version of missing children on milk cartons. Now, if it all ended tomorrow, so what? I printed out a color copy of the circular Mayan calendar and marked off what I thought were the days—how can anyone read one of those things?—until December 21, 2012, when the world would end. Then it would be out of my hands. I awoke December 22 disappointed and still here. I torched the lame calendar.

I toyed with returning to school to get another master's degree or a PhD. Learning always made me happy. Perhaps I could become a career student. But if I did live to be one hundred, even though I'd still be coloring my gray hair light brown, I'd be paying off student loans while a resident in a nursing home.

This bad humor was unlike me, and though I constantly searched myself for its cause, I couldn't pinpoint the origin. Without a cause, I had no clue how to fix it. I considered seeing my doctor, who probably would have prescribed antidepressants, even though I didn't feel depressed. I had never believed it was good medicine to treat symptoms and not the cause. Therapy was another option. But a funk didn't warrant dredging up my past, blaming my parents, or exploring any more of my emotions.

I was grieving.

I had lost my purpose.

Of course, it would be silly to tell you that one event made me a happy person again and that this one event gave my life purpose, a goal, a mission. Yet, one nutty idea that began with "How hard can it be?" started me on a journey I had never expected to take. I was the last person on the planet anyone would expect to embark on, of all things, a spiritual quest. And one that would lead me to find a little-known religion. Even I gagged at the thought.

I am embarrassed to admit what prompted this whole thing. (Don't laugh, okay?) One night as I flipped through TV stations, a woman with bleached-white hair, French-manicured talons, and an unmistakable Long Island accent caught my attention. Theresa Caputo, the *Long Island Medium*, channeled dead people on the screen.

Even though I'd always been fascinated with the paranormal, I was, to some degree, a skeptic. I knew there wasn't much reality in reality TV. Years ago, I watched a show about a pet psychic. Everything she said that the dog or cat "told" her, I could have known by studying animal behavior. I scrutinized the *Long Island Medium* with the same level of skepticism. But Theresa seemed to deliver bizarre details that only the person she did the reading for and the departed could have known.

My partner, Jim, and I have been talking with the dead for three decades—as professional genealogists. We channeled long-forgotten ancestors by digging up historical documents they'd left behind and reassembling the pieces of their lives, recreating their life stories. But wouldn't it be cool if I could become a medium and actually talk to those dead ancestors and get answers? The stubborn ones could *tell* me where to find them in the records. They could put me on the right track in telling their life stories.

So, on a whim and with no plans for my six-week winter break from teaching online, I decided to be a "stunt journalist." I'd be the Nellie Bly of mediumship. Instead of going undercover in an insane asylum (then again, maybe that's closer to where I belonged), I'd immerse myself in the world of mediumship to see if anyone—anyone average like me in her mid-fifties with no prior, youthful psychic, visionary, or near-death experiences—could not only talk to the dead, but get a response.

And that's how it all started. That's the nutty idea that would now give my life purpose. Perhaps even nuttier was that Jim fully supported me when I announced my new project. We sat at the kitchen table, drinking mugs of hot tea on a frosty December morning. It was still dark outside, but I could see through the sliding glass door a dusting of snow on the patio. I pulled my fleece bathrobe tighter around me. "I've decided I'm going to become a medium and really talk to the dead," I said. There was no look of surprise on his morning-stubble face. His short, graying hair didn't stand on end. And his implanted pacemaker/defibrillator didn't jolt and resuscitate him.

"Oh. Okay," he said.

We had just gotten up, so maybe he wasn't fully awake yet. Normally I'm the one who has to have the caffeine from my black tea surging through my veins before I'm coherent, let alone alert enough to make such a proclamation. I explained I'd been watching the *Long Island Medium*, and it made me wonder whether anyone could become a medium. "Really, how hard can it be?" I said. Jim knew me well enough to know that when I said that, I had made up my mind.

Jim was almost ten years older than I and closer to death's door, so perhaps this would give us both some peace of mind, knowing we'd still be able to communicate when the time came for one of us to leave this world. He told me he'd always believed in an afterlife, good Catholic boy that he was growing up, but neither of us had ever entertained the idea of going to a medium or actually trying to communicate with the other side.

Jim, in his kelly-green Ireland sweatshirt with a shamrock in the center, took a sip of tea, then grinned and said, "You amaze me with the things you come up with, but nothing surprises me anymore."

"I'm giving it a year," I told him, my hands cupping the mug for warmth. I would become a medium—or not—within one year, then write about my journey. You don't know me well enough yet, but I'm a quick study and an impatient person. Even a year sounded like a long-term goal to me. In fact, if patience was the primary lesson I was supposed to learn in this lifetime, I wouldn't be graduating with my class. I was all about the destination, not the journey. Are we there yet? But when some bizarre, unexpected, and devastating things happened, I learned it really was about the journey.

CHAPTER 1

I'll Miss You When You're Gone

"I found a way out of my funk," I told Laurie, my only child, over the phone on a frigid Sunday afternoon after I'd made my decision to become a medium. I sat at my desk in a corner of our condo's living room in Salt Lake City, Utah, my computer screen open to Theresa Captuo's website, reading her bio, while I talked. Laurie lived in Oregon and had just had her first baby the previous August. She was on winter break from teaching at the local high school. She must have been holding my granddaughter; I could hear her gurgling in the background.

"I'm going to become a medium and talk to dead people." I made it sound as normal as if I had taken up bird watching.

"Oh," Laurie said. I was certain she could hear the excitement in my voice. I could certainly hear the dismay in hers.

"What do you think?"

"Umm . . ." My normally loquacious Laurie seemed stymied. "I thought you wanted to be a lion tamer."

I rolled my eyes. "That was several glasses of wine ago."

I didn't tell her the other part of the story—that I was scared. Of death.

Not of dying, actually. But afraid of the grief and loss it causes. Already this new endeavor had unleashed in me a fear I didn't realize I had.

I'd always had an unconventional relationship with death and the dead. I hadn't been personally touched by death until my twenty-fifth year when the only grandmother I knew passed away from heart disease at age seventy-six. At the wake in the funeral home in Southern California, it was an open, silver casket. Even though I hadn't seen her in a few years, she looked the same as I remembered her: a round, unwrinkled face with fine red capillaries on her cheeks, and perfectly manicured red fingernails. Pretty nails were always important to her, and she loved giving me manicures because I could grow long fingernails, too. She'd snip and file the tips of my nails to uneven triangular points, and when she applied the polish, she never painted the half-moons. I thought she made my nails look goofy, but the same style worked on her. For a woman who stood not quite five feet tall, she had large hands with sizeable nail beds. My hands and nails were petite. When she'd finish my manicures, my nails looked like blood-tipped daggers.

This was my first wake, and it turned out to be more comical than somber. I mostly remember the huge debate among my Italian-American relatives about whether Grandma should have her glasses on or not.

"She doesn't look right without them," one relative said.

"But she's got her eyes closed," said another.

"Who wears glasses with their eyes closed?"

I might have said, "We can open them."

During the wake, my dad, bored from standing around and looking at his dead mother in a viewing room the size of a spare bedroom, took me in search of the casket showroom. We oohed and aahed over the shiny new models as if they were Cadillacs that had just rolled off the assembly line.

When I hung out my shingle as a professional genealogist in 1988 at the age of thirty-two, I dealt with death and the dead on a daily basis. I had become enamored with dead relatives when I was about ten, when friends of my parents we visited in rural New York took me to an old graveyard to look at the carved skulls and crossbones on colonial headstones. A (live) man in the cemetery was there copying down headstone inscriptions, and he explained that he was a genealogist and told me how to get started tracing my family tree. The rest is history—literally. (I wrote about this experience in my essay collection *Inheriting the Gordon Hips*.)

In my twenties, after I took a local genealogy class, I became serious about researching my ancestors, and a decade later, I found my tribe when I attended my first national genealogical conference and decided to turn pro. I discovered only another genealogist could share and understand my enthusiasm when a death certificate arrived in the mail, or relate to the elation over discovering an ancestor had succumbed in a particularly gruesome passing. This meant the ancestor's demise would have made the papers, and there'd be a coroner's report and maybe an inquest, too. More records to find! Short death notices were disappointments; long obituaries gave me pleasure.

Genealogists get excited when we "kill off" ancestors, which means we have a concrete date to look for a will, probate packet, or an obituary. We're saddened that our great-great-grandmother lost half of her children to illness, accidents, and pestilence, but that also focuses us on tracing the children who survived into adulthood. We hang out in cemeteries. The dead don't haunt us; we haunt them. We have picnics at family plots, visiting our ancestors and eating our lunches as if in a public park, just as our ancestors did a century or so ago. The only thing missing for us is the barbeque pit. Our kids mount and climb gravestones as if the cemetery were one huge jungle gym.

Genealogists will scale stone walls or ascend chain-linked fences, brave overgrown weed patches possibly infested with snakes, break rusty locks to enter mausoleums, and risk limbs walking uneven ground where graves have sunk, all in the quest for locating dead relations. I remember when one colleague came to a genealogy conference on crutches. "What happened?" we asked and then listened enraptured as she told us how she tripped over a recessed grave marker and broke her leg. "Wow. That is so cool!" We smiled and wore our envy and pride for her on our sleeves. We revered our comrade as if she'd recently returned from the front and her war injury had earned her a Purple Heart. Visiting final resting places is the only reason genealogists leave the comforts of a library, archive, or courthouse, or venture away from our home computer screens. Genealogists have the time of our lives with all the records a death creates because it's more documentation of a person's life.

Death, for me, had never been anything to fear. I knew that one day a baby genealogist would come along and find the same joy in my death as I found in my ancestors'. Death for me was abstract, nothing frightening; it occurred on documents housed in repositories or on tombstones in graveyards.

I didn't fear dying so much as I feared leaving my daughter and my partner. I've enjoyed a life of control—what I called "helping"—and I wasn't sure whether they'd know what to do with all my stuff, what items held meaning for me that they should keep, and which could go in the trash or to Goodwill. Or if they'd care. Thomas Lynch, a mortician who wrote *The Undertaking: Life Studies from the Dismal Trade*, says that "the dead don't care," but they do, if you believe in an afterlife. How frustrating will it be to hover over Jim and Laurie's heads as they sort through my belongings? I'll be unable to communicate with them and will be frantically waving my transparent spirit arms with my well-manicured fingernails when they pitch my great-grandmother's rolling pin—yet keep the one I bought at Walmart.

I also couldn't bear the thought of leaving Laurie. We'd always had a close mother-daughter bond. I didn't want to miss out on any of her adult life as she raised her kids and grew older. That really frightened me about death. If death was truly *fini*, as some people believe, then I wouldn't be there when Laurie needed her mom to talk to. I wouldn't be able to comfort her during the time she needs me the most: as grief washes over her after my death. I wouldn't be able to tell her that she'll be fine, that she has always been the best part of me, that I've worshipped and adored her. And that I wasn't the wind beneath her wings—she was the wind beneath mine. I believed she knew this, but it wouldn't be the same telling her these things while I'm still alive. Laurie would say, "Aw. That's really sweet of you to say, Mommy." She doesn't like to think of her parents dying. That's not a reality she is ready to face. It's after death, during the stages of grief, when she'll need to hear this from me.

Loss terrified me. I lost a favorite pencil once and thought I'd go mad with grief. I use Paper Mate's Sharpwriter #2 yellow mechanical pencils, which you'd think would be easy to replace. But on some of the pencils, the lead feels too hard and scratchy on paper, or the erasers aren't soft and leave a black smudge when you try to erase something. This particular pencil had the perfect combination of lead and eraser. To distinguish it from any imposters, I had dressed it with a hot-pink foam grip, which had conformed to my fingers alone. I had been working in bed, and without warning, my beloved pencil disappeared. I searched for it behind the bed and under it. I shook out the quilt.

Jim must have unconsciously pilfered it, I reasoned. He has a tendency to do that. I don't like to remind him of it, but under that full head of silver hair, he is rather forgetful. I made him look for it on and in his nightstand, on and in his desk, in his computer bag, where he sits at the kitchen table, and in his bathroom. Nothing. It seemed to have vanished into thin air. I checked there, too. Nope. It hadn't lodged itself into the ceiling. I hunted for it on and around the bed every day, longing for my lost pencil, checking under the pillows and inside the cases, too. I got on my hands and knees and looked under the bed with a flashlight. "Oh, hi, Figaro. What are you doing under there?" When I reached for him, it turned out I was petting a cat-sized dust ball. I really needed new glasses. And a cleaning lady. But still no pencil. Where could it have gone?

When I found the damn thing a week later nestled between the sheets at the foot of the bed, I was so ecstatic, you would have thought I'd found the Lost Ark of the Covenant. So let us pause for a moment to imagine how I would cope with the loss of a loved one . . .

By the time I turned fifty-six, I had lost my mother and two close friends. One was my best friend, and even though it had been three years, I missed her as much as if she had died only yesterday. Because my mother and I had had a stormy relationship most of our lives, and we weren't especially close, I didn't think losing her would affect me as much as it did. But I cried daily, nightly, and at the mere thought of her for weeks after her passing. I hadn't lost just my mother but the archivist of my childhood history. And I felt guilty for the way I had ignored her and for the way I'd treated her when I wasn't ignoring her.

Our problems went back to my teens, probably earlier. I was an only child, Daddy's little girl, and quite spoiled. I remember yelling at my mother when she'd discipline me, "I don't like you!" She'd calmly reply, "You don't have to like me. You just have to tolerate me." So that's what I did.

Yes, there were times when the storms lifted, but it was a fair-weather relationship. When I was little, I'd call, "Mommy! Mommy! Mommy!" to get her attention. Busy with something, she wouldn't even turn around when she said, "I changed my name." Then I spent an hour trying to figure out her new name. "Is it Ann?" "No." "Is it Suzie?" "No." "Is it Kathy?" "No." And on it would go. A professional seamstress, my mom taught me how to sew when I was about ten. She helped me make a flannel nightgown for myself, although I'm quite certain she must have sewn in the sleeves. I was a chubby child, and in sixth grade when I noticed boys for the first time, she became my personal trainer, helping me manage my eating habits ("What do you mean no more bread and potatoes? And no Hostess cupcakes? What kind of torture is this?")

and exercising with me to Jack LaLanne on television after school. She probably feared I'd never leave home if I didn't lose weight by junior high.

My father divorced my mother while I was in my teens. I'd heard, although I have no memory of from whom, that it bothered him that my mother looked older than he did. She was red haired, fair complected, and a smoker. I can't recall a time when she wasn't wrinkled, although her skin was always soft. I loved touching her cheeks when I was a child. My Italian-American father had olive skin and pitch-black hair. Like a fine Italian wine, his looks improved with age. In their wedding photo, they looked happy, of course, but clearly things soured somewhat quickly. My mother told me he hit her—once. She left with me in my stroller. He came after her, and never hit her again.

When they divorced, I expected I would be given the choice of where I wanted to live, which was to live with him. When that wasn't the case, I blamed her for my unhappiness. In my junior year of high school, my mother moved the two of us away from all my friends, and, more importantly, the boyfriend I'd lost my virginity to, so she could be closer to her family in New York. Because she also suffered from "nervous breakdowns," I now felt the burden of being her caregiver. I should have been angry with my father over this, but in my eyes, he could do no wrong. I didn't realize or understand that he was most likely the cause of her nervous condition due to his mental abuse of her.

Once I turned eighteen, I moved in with my father and his new wife. I'd like to tell you that, with distance and maturity, things with my mom improved, and to a degree they did, but it was never an easy comradery. Over the years, I had marinated in my resentment. As she had told me long ago, I didn't have to like her; I just had to tolerate her. A clever statement that backfired.

Fast-forward seventeen years to when Laurie was in fourth grade. Her father and I moved to Simla, a small town on the eastern plains of

Colorado, in the mid-1990s. And when I say small, I mean small. The population within the town limits contained about three hundred—or five hundred, if you counted the surrounding ranches and the cows. Mom retired and moved to Simla, too, to be closer to her only child and only grandchild. She lived in a one-bedroom house on a side lane north of the highway. Our house sat on one of the main roads several blocks over on the south side of the highway.

I included her in my weekly shopping trips to Colorado Springs, forty-five miles away, and we made a day of it, eating lunch at Panera Bread. Those outings were good for us both; all I needed to do was focus on her and our shopping lists. But I worked from home, and back there, I easily lost patience with her for just being her. Her voice grated on me. Her phone calls interrupted whatever I was doing and annoyed me. I begrudged giving up my time to take her to doctors' appointments. The doctor and nurses would tell me I was such a "good daughter" for taking care of her. They didn't know I did it out of obligation, nothing more.

In the spring of 2004, eastern Colorado experienced a nasty blizzard. We'd had several inches of snow already, and it blew as if God had taken a huge deep breath and exhaled. There was no visibility. By this time, I was divorced, Laurie was on her own, and Jim now lived with me. We had just finished dinner and were cleaning up when Mom called to say she had fallen and couldn't get up. "Can Jim come over and help me?" she asked.

I don't know exactly what triggered my sudden outburst—her needy voice, her imposition on our time, her existence—but years of pent-up resentment came out all at once.

"Are you crazy? We're in the middle of a fucking blizzard!" I yelled into the phone on my kitchen wall, spewing the venom of a viper, my fangs unhinged to strike.

Jim heard my response and motioned to me. I covered the mouthpiece and told him what she wanted.

"I'll walk over there," he said. I was stunned, but not surprised. Jim was a rescuer. He thrived on helping and taking care of others. That's what I loved about him. He took good care of me, although after my explosion, he was probably eager to get away from the firestorm.

We knew he wouldn't be able to drive as the roads hadn't been plowed yet and were impassible.

"Are you crazy, too?" I asked him. "What if you slip and fall and break something? What if the wind knocks you down?" We had no cell phone service in this rural part of Colorado. "No, you aren't going."

He insisted. A Minnesotan accustomed to snow, he put on his coat, gloves, boots, and knit cap.

I took my hand off the phone receiver and told my mother Jim was on his way. I screeched like an angry owl into the phone, although she probably could have heard me without the phone, "He's on his way. And he's walking! If anything happens to him, I will never forgive you!"

Jim headed out the door while I continued to yell at my mom on the phone. "Why couldn't you just call 911 and get the volunteer firefighters to come? Make sure he calls me the minute he gets there!" I slammed down the receiver.

I know. Shameful. Like an only-child spoiled brat. Which I was. I should have been grateful that when she fell, she didn't break anything or knock herself unconscious; she could crawl to the phone for help. But I wasn't grateful. I only thought of the inconvenience it caused and the thought of losing Jim.

He made it there safely, helped her up, warmed up a bit, then walked back home in the blizzard. When he walked in the door and I hugged him, I worried he'd crack from being frozen.

To this day, I can't believe I screamed at my mother like that. I can't believe I wasn't more compassionate and caring. I can't believe I wasn't more humane and self-sacrificing like Jim. It became my biggest regret. And my biggest lesson about how selfish I could be.

I did admire Mom's mischievous and sarcastic side, though. With heart and balance problems and severe osteoporosis, she was forced to move into a nursing home in Simla—just two doors down from my house. She wasn't happy, of course, and wanted to live with me. But by then, she had gained a lot of weight, and there was no way Jim and I could lift her if she fell. My once red-headed, tall, and thin mother was now short, chubby, graying, and curled like a boiled shrimp inside a walker. After she settled into her new surroundings, she decided to offer her sage and unsolicited advice to one new resident. The lady claimed she wouldn't be there long, that she'd be going home soon. While they sat at dinner together, my mother informed her, "The only way out of here is in a hearse."

My mother also developed a knack for waking the dead. After that, another woman was assigned to her dining table, a lady slumped in a wheelchair who had been near-catatonic for months. But after one meal with my mother relentlessly nagging her to eat, the woman came to life and spoke to the nursing home director: "Move me to another table!"

Jim and I decided to move to Salt Lake City. We were making more frequent and longer trips there for our clients to do research at the Family History Library, the world's largest genealogical library. We determined it was better to leave Mom in Simla, where by then she knew everyone in the small, twenty-four bed nursing home. But making trips back to Colorado to visit her several times a year became costly and took us away from our work. When we had traveled to Salt Lake, we could write the trips off as business expenses, but that wasn't the case in reverse. I grew to resent spending all our Christmases with her, eating a holiday dinner of pale, limp, canned green beans, dried-out ham, and a potato casserole with enough cheese to clog a rhinoceros's arteries. It's said that once someone goes into a nursing home, their life expectancy is only about two years. I didn't doubt it. I'd eaten the food.

I longed for the day when I wouldn't have to spend my Christmas breaks on the road to be with her instead of at home or with my daughter. After Mom died in 2011, the first Christmas without that burden was bittersweet and more somber than I had expected. I didn't miss the nursing home food, but I missed my mom's laughter as Jim and I joked and teased with her over the meal.

As time passed, I didn't mourn her death as I initially did. But I had trouble accepting that nothing but memories and material things survive. I had trouble accepting that what mostly remains are guilt and regrets.

I was so fearful of losing Jim. I've relied on him for so many of my daily emotional needs and sanity. He's not just the person I'm in love with, but he's my best friend, my support system, my person. When I tell him I love him, I often add, "I'll miss you when you're gone." He laughs when I say this, but he doesn't realize that this is not something I've ever said to anyone else. I certainly never said it to my ex-husband.

Jim and I met at the first genealogical conference I attended in 1989. His hair then was nearly all black and quite thick, which he wore in a neat, standard men's haircut. Hair is usually the first thing I notice about someone. We were both married, and it would be some fourteen years later, when I was in my mid-forties, and he in his mid-fifties, that our harmless flirting turned serious. By then, we had both mentally checked out of our marriages for reasons that had nothing to do with one another. We just hadn't gotten to that little pesky detail of divorcing our spouses yet, but that soon followed when Jim and I realized we had more in common than our failing marriages.

I'd melt when Jim smiled and winked at me. I loved that he was a deep, philosophical thinker, recommending books to me such as Thomas Moore's *The Re-Enchantment of Everyday Life*. My deep, philosophical thinking extended only as far as wondering what kind of salad I'd make with the grilled chicken for dinner. Giving me flowers wasn't just for a special occasion to Jim but because it was Tuesday and he loved me. I adored inhaling his clean, masculine scent; he wasn't one to use colognes, which to me indicated someone who didn't hide behind anything artificial. Sure, he had his flaws, as did I. He brought with him to the relationship a life-threatening health problem, cardiomyopathy, an enlarged heart muscle that doesn't pump blood efficiently. He was diagnosed at age forty-four in 1992, and, at the time, his life expectancy was five years. He long ago beat those odds, and an implanted pacemaker/defibrillator eleven years later reduced his risk of sudden death by 90 percent. But his health scares didn't end there. A few years later, in 2008, Jim developed early-stage prostate cancer. Neither one of us worried much about the prostate cancer, though, because the doctor was most reassuring. He said that Jim's heart would kill him long before the cancer would.

Still, because of his health conditions, the odds were good that I would outlive Jim. I knew we'd never celebrate a golden anniversary. Ever since we've been a couple, I've asked the Universe nightly that we get at least twenty years together, preferably more, of course. What will I do without the person who's so deeply burrowed into my heart? Without the daily laughter we share? Without the teasing and fun banter we love and appreciate about each other? Without my soul mate? No matter how much time we have, it will be too little, and that scares me.

It didn't take long for me to realize that this engulfing fear—that death might be the final curtain, that once a person has died nothing remains for the living but memories and material things—might actually be the root of my funk and the genesis for my journey to become a medium. I didn't want to merely believe in an afterlife. I wanted to *know* with certainty.

Henry Wadsworth Longfellow's poem, "Resignation," says,

> There is no Death! What seems so is transition;
> This life of mortal breath
> Is but a suburb of the life elysian,
> Whose portal we call Death.

Was death only a transition and portal to a different reality? Was it possible to communicate with deceased relatives and ancestors? Could Jim and I still be close when he departs this life? That's what I intended to find out.

CHAPTER 2

A Psychic Fraud

Back in the sixties, I was enamored of all things *Dark Shadows*—Barnabas Collins loomed green each night in a glow-in-the-dark poster thumbtacked to the glittery ceiling above my bed. *Bewitched's* Samantha Stephens entered my life, too, and I practiced for hours in front of the mirror, trying to twitch my nose like Samantha. I was fairly confident I wouldn't be able to perform magic, but that was okay. I went for the cute factor. It's like when a guy wiggles his ears. It's cute, and you can't help but stare and say, "Do it again."

As I entered my freshman year of high school, declaring myself a witch was an attention-getter, a way to be noticed. When my nose-twitching ability wouldn't materialize, I moved on to the more mundane aspects of practicing witchcraft: burning candles and casting spells. I dubbed Boris, my black cat, a familiar. I wore my long, brunette hair straight and parted down the middle. I dressed in mostly black clothing accessorized with a silver pentagram necklace. My mother, who made most of my clothes, didn't say anything when all the fabric I picked out was one shade of black. I had broken her heart when I told her I no longer believed in God, and I'm sure she must've wondered how her chubby, cherubic daughter went from wanting to be a nun clothed in black garb to an atheist teen clothed in black garb.

Both of my parents were Catholic, so naturally, I had been raised Catholic. Each Saturday morning of my elementary school years, my mother dropped me off at the parish school in La Mirada, California, where I attended catechism classes taught by nuns in black habits. I wasn't sure why I had to go there on Saturdays plus go to Mass on Sunday mornings. Wasn't sacrificing sleeping in one morning a week good enough for God? None of my friends at school were Catholic, so I didn't know anyone at catechism. I was an only child who didn't make friends easily, and seeing my Catholic comrades only once a week made it even more difficult to form bonds. To this day, about all I can remember from catechism was when one nun, Sister Mary Something-or-other, threw her hands and papers up in the air when someone knocked on the classroom door and interrupted her lesson for about the third time. "Doors, doors, doors!" she said. For some reason, we thought that was the funniest thing a nun had ever said. It probably was.

When I saw *The Trouble with Angels* on the big screen in 1966 at the age of ten, I decided I wanted to be a nun when I grew up. What could be more fun than being a nun, or better yet, the mother superior, at an all-girls Catholic boarding school with rebellious, hormonal teenagers? The sisters looked serene and as if they enjoyed life, despite the spirited young women in their charge. And Silent Sunday seemed like heaven to me: a whole day of not speaking to anyone and no one speaking to me. Maybe I'd join a silent order.

As a child, I liked Mass well enough, partly for the rituals, but mostly because I got to see my mom and dad together and dressed up. It was the only time I remembered seeing my father in a suit, usually plain black with a white dress shirt and skinny black tie. It was also the only time I saw both of them in a complete state of reverence. My mother knelt in her hip-tight dress, bowed her head with the white lace doily bobby-pinned to her red hair, and thudded her left breast with her right fist each time the priest rang bells. As she thumped her fist over her heart, she also nodded when she murmured, "Jesus." Why she did this was a mystery; they didn't teach us that in catechism class.

My black-haired, Italian-American father often served as an usher, so Mom and I always sat at the end of a pew, forcing people to climb in and over us while we saved him a seat. He'd leave the pew toward the end of Mass to get the basket on the long pole to collect donations row by row. Then came my favorite part of the Mass—well, actually my second favorite. My favorite part was going home. I'd sit up tall, crane my neck to see between and around the people in front of me, and beam as my dad genuflected in sync with the other usher when they brought the offering up to the altar and handed the baskets to the priest. I later learned that my father had been an altar boy most of his youth and that he had wanted to become a priest. That ambition ended in high school when the teacher caught him doodling nude images of women. Thank goodness he wasn't doodling nude images of priests and altar boys.

Church for a kid like me wasn't a place of worship or prayer but an opportunity to explore the contents of my mother's pocketbook, inhaling the smell of her Chesterfields when I twisted opened the double-clasp latch. Mass was where I learned that skin is elastic. I'd gently pinch—after Mom slapped me once for pinching too hard—a layer of skin from the back of her hand and watch it slink back into place. Mass was where whiffs of my dad's Old Spice aftershave comforted me as I leaned against him. Mass held fond childhood memories of my parents, but no profound enlightenment.

During my first confession—a requirement before making my first Holy Communion—I was terrified that the other kids in my catechism class could hear me in the confessional while they waited in line for their turn. I have no recollection of what I confessed, but what could I have possibly done that required God's forgiveness or He wouldn't let me into heaven? I was seven, for Chrissake. But just the thought of someone overhearing me confess, as well as having to tell a strange man what an evil person I was, caused me to vow that I'd never sin again. Or I would keep my indiscretions to myself. Apparently, that's what my parents had decided, too. As reverent as they were, I don't recall ever seeing them go to confession or receiving communion. I figured if they hadn't been struck by lightning yet for not accepting the body and blood of Christ, the odds must be in my favor. Besides, the bland communion wafer—couldn't they have added just a touch of salt?—plastered itself to the roof of my mouth, and it was all I could do to sit in the pew and not pry the damn thing off with my finger.

When my father took a job as a helicopter pilot for the Environmental Protection Agency's project to survey pollution in some twelve hundred lakes all over the country, he was on the road much of the time. So just Mom and I attended Mass. By then, we had relocated to Las Vegas, Nevada. I was now in my early teens and questioning "the mysteries of faith," to which no one seemed to have any logical answers. If God created the world in seven days and man on the sixth day, where do the dinosaurs fit in? If Adam and Eve were the only people on the planet, and they had just two sons, with whom did Cain mate? His mother? If the Immaculate Conception took place on December 8, how is it possible for Mary to give birth on December 25? Even as bad as I was at math, I knew that made no sense. And how was it that Mary was married to Joseph but she was still a virgin? Didn't Joseph raise an eyebrow when she announced she was pregnant? These small Biblical discrepancies troubled a teen like me, who was beginning to think for herself. I hadn't even considered the larger, more philosophical issues yet.

Since my dad was no longer around to enforce church attendance, I decided I didn't need to go and told my mother I wasn't going to Mass anymore. I don't recall whether my mother went alone, but she stopped going altogether when she and my father divorced. The church deemed divorce a sin, and she wouldn't be welcomed at Mass again.

I didn't tell my mother that I practiced witchcraft. She'd suffered several "nervous breakdowns" during my childhood and teen years. I never knew her official diagnosis, but I could tell when she started to lose her grip on reality. Her voice became higher pitched, almost childlike, and she'd say things that made no sense. There was no reasoning with her. She was in her own world. On a few occasions, she had to be hospitalized and was medicated, probably with antipsychotics and antidepressants. I remember visiting her each time just a couple of days after she was admitted, and she would already be back to her usual self. Whatever they gave her worked quickly.

I didn't know anything then about mental illness, and I had no idea what triggered her episodes. I saw her nervousness and breaks with reality as a weakness, assuming that she wasn't emotionally strong enough to cope with life's daily challenges. My mother was an embarrassment for me. I didn't know that, as a child, she had witnessed her aunt, with whom she lived and whom she thought of as a mother, being physically abused by her uncle, her aunt screaming and pleading for mercy. I didn't know then that this uncle had her aunt committed, and she underwent electroconvulsive (electroshock) therapy. I didn't know then that my father emotionally abused my mother, and that probably her greatest fear was ending up like her aunt.

All I knew was my mother had to be treated like a porcelain doll, one that could easily shatter. I didn't want to be the cause of another episode. She wouldn't understand my new interest.

I don't recall how I discovered and ordered books on witchcraft— there was no Amazon then. But back when I practiced witchcraft in the early 1970s, there were basically four types of witches: white, gray, black, and, of course, kitchen witches who magically prevented pots from boiling over. White witches believed in a god and were faith healers. Since I wasn't sure whether there was a God, and I had no healing powers, I didn't claim to be a white witch. Black witches practiced black magic and cast harmful spells on people. That didn't sit right with me. Gray witches believed in neutrality, harmony, and balance; they recognized and respected other's beliefs, but they didn't feel the need for an anchor like a church.

I learned these oversimplified definitions from a phonograph album I ordered by mail called *Barbara, The Gray Witch*, so I called myself a gray witch. In some ways, I followed the Wiccan religion—a pagan belief in witchcraft and rituals—but I didn't belong to a coven, nor did I know anyone who believed as I did. I practiced magic by burning candles and incense, reciting spells and incantations, reading tarot cards, and tossing *I Ching* divination coins. Occasionally, I consulted my Magic 8 Ball just for validation. I believed—simply because I wanted to; I had no evidence of it—that there was an afterlife in the form of earthbound ghosts and spirits who reincarnated. It's said, though, that you shouldn't try to conjure the dead. No problem. It would scare me to death if I did.

I had, and still do have, this conflicting desire to be liked and the same as everyone else yet independent and unique. Standing out too far from the norm, though, meant that you were weird, or worse, a dweeb. But goth-hood was still in its infancy in the sixties and seventies; it was mysterious and cool. I wasn't part of the popular crowd in high school, but boys found me curious, and the girls—my competition and the ones who might have otherwise ignored me—wanted to know if I would cast love spells for them on the boys they had crushes on. My mail-order, black leather-bound spell book and I were in demand. There I was in the kitchen after school, my mother at work, casting spells. I lit a red tapered candle I had bought at Kmart, wrote my girlfriends' love intentions on a piece of paper, burned it in one of my mother's saucepans, and chanted the love spell in the book.

I knew I was a fraud, a charlatan, a sheep in wolf's clothing. After I "saw" *The Exorcist* (I hid my eyes through 99 percent of the movie), I slept with the lights on for weeks. "Tubular Bells," the theme music, gave me the willies—still does. I had to shut off the radio every time it played. I was no more psychic than a brick. The only past life I remembered occurred yesterday. No apparition ever stood at the foot of my bed. (It's always at the foot.) I once asked my mother if I'd ever had an "imaginary friend." She said I used to talk to the little girl in the mirror—me. I couldn't conjure the dead to save my life, and I never could make that stupid plastic planchette indicator move over the Ouija board by myself. Which was just as well. I was afraid of ghosts, too.

I used my "powers" to make friends and get boyfriends. If a spell worked, it was sheer coincidence. If a curse came true, it was because I'd told someone I placed a curse on them. When anything remotely bad happened to them during the next few days—and the odds were in my favor—they'd blame it on the curse and beg me to remove the spell. That was my "power." More than witchcraft, I practiced psychology.

My high school English teacher, who didn't judge my rebellious nature toward mainstream religion, brought to my attention Mark Twain's *Letters from the Earth*. Finally, I thought as I read it, there is a sane and rational individual revered in the annals of literature who makes sense of this whole God and religion nonsense. Letter II made a particular impact on me—the report on how humans envisioned heaven. Twain pointed out the irony that humans place sexual intercourse above all other pleasures, "yet he has left it out of his heaven! . . . prayer takes its place." In heaven, wrote Twain, everyone sings the same hymn over and over, and everyone also plays the harp, creating a "deafening hurricane of sound—millions and millions of voices screaming at once and millions and millions of harps" playing at the same time. To top that off, heaven is a never-ending church service; yet on earth, humans can barely tolerate an hour of it once a week. Unlike here on earth where everyone hates one another, in heaven, everyone gets along, no matter what their nationality, religion, politics, or race.

If heaven was indeed as humans envisioned it, or worse yet, as Mark Twain described it—and it sounded pretty awful to me—I decided I'd take my chances in hell. My only concern was whether there would be a power outlet for my electric blanket when I arrived there. I've always been chilly at night no matter where I was.

I stopped calling myself a witch after high school—although some people I know might still call me that, or worse. My adult world was peopled with conservatives and Christians, and trying to explain my magic beliefs made me stand too far out. After I gave birth to Laurie in my mid-twenties, I gave the Catholic Church another try, figuring some seventy-five million people in the United States couldn't all be wrong. I wanted my daughter to have some religion in her upbringing, and Catholicism was familiar. The Sunday I decided to attend Mass again happened to be the end of daylight saving time when we were supposed to turn the clocks back an hour. I arrived in time to hear the priest say, "Go in peace." Maybe that was a sign.

The next Sunday I arrived at the correct time, only to discover some things in the Mass had changed in the past decade and a half. I'd still been attending Mass after the Vatican II changes in the sixties, so I knew that the priest would be facing the congregation rather than having his back to us. I also knew that I no longer needed to wear a doily on my head. But when we came to reciting the Lord's Prayer, things went horribly awry. In unison with the others, my confidence growing that I remembered the words, I said the last line I'd learned, "and deliver us from evil," then bellowed a punctuated "Amen." But the congregation kept going. When had they added, "For thine is the kingdom, and the power, and the glory, for ever and ever"?

I had taken a seat in a back pew by the door, reserved for those who sneak out during communion, so I could observe and not attract any attention. After the debacle with the Lord's Prayer, I felt self-conscious and tried to make myself as small as possible by burying my nose in the Catholic missal and trying to determine what other changes might be afoot. Then the priest asked everyone to exchange a sign of peace by greeting each other and shaking hands. Huh? This was going too far. I wasn't here to talk to *people*. I was here to talk to God. And what I liked most about Him was He didn't talk back.

Yet, even with these changes and a "choir" that consisted of a Peter-Paul-and-Mary-type ensemble, I hung in there for a few more weeks. When one homily revolved around the parish's financial status, complete with transparency graphs on an overhead projector, that was enough for me. This wasn't the Catholic Church I knew. I came there for the ritual and spiritual enlightenment, not a lesson in guilt over the sorry state of parish economics.

A close friend was a born-again Christian, and for a while, I attended an evangelical church with her. Laurie's father had no interest in attending any church services with me, but I felt it was important for Laurie to have some religious exposure, so I sent her to the evangelical vacation Bible school one summer for a week when she was about four. I figured it couldn't hurt her, even though the Christian religion now felt to me like wearing a scratchy wool turtleneck sweater in August.

I considered the Bible a parabolic work of fiction but thought that stories that teach life's lessons could do no harm, whether they're *Fables of Aesop*, *Grimms' Fairy Tales*, or the Bible. The way I saw it, the men who wrote the Old Testament portrayed God mostly as angry, vengeful, and punitive. Let's face it, he's not a terribly nice dude, and he has a lot of conditions to his love. When the New Testament came along, those writers realized that every "villain" needs a "hero." Enter the son of God, Jesus. He's the loving, compassionate, healing "character," whom Christians seem to worship over God, not surprisingly. But God's the jealous type who said, "Thou shalt have no other gods before me." God's son, however, well, that's another story.

I couldn't tolerate that scratchy wool turtleneck for long. At one service at the evangelical church, the minister insisted the Mormon religion was a cult and we must shun Mormons at all costs. As a genealogist with many Mormon friends, I took offense. Some of their beliefs and restrictions might be different from mine, but so were those of the Jewish faith. Were they a cult, too? Weren't we supposed to have unconditional love and compassion for all?

Then, at the Christmas Eve service, the minister took it upon himself to announce to the congregation, which included children, that there was no Santa Claus. I never returned to that church or rarely any other. I wasn't going to tolerate such child abuse. Fortunately, six-year-old Laurie, engrossed in exploring the contents of her mother's purse at the time, wasn't paying attention, so she continued to believe in Santa until her senior year in high school.

CHAPTER 3

Finding Guidance

For my fortieth birthday, my (then) husband and I spent the night in the Lizzie Borden house on Second Street in Fall River, Massachusetts. The three-story rectangular house, painted olive green with a darker green trim, was where Lizzie allegedly gave her stepmother forty whacks with an axe and her father forty-one. It had been turned into a bed-and-breakfast. Long a fan of Lizzie's, I couldn't think of a better way to commemorate my birthday. The toughest decision was whether to book the room where Lizzie's stepmother, Abby, was whacked to death or to stay in Lizzie's bedroom. I opted for Lizzie's room.

It was October 1996, mid-week, and off season, so my husband and I had the whole house to ourselves. Upon arrival, our host and tour guide showed us around the eight-room house, stopping to explain who occupied each room and what had happened that night. We were free to take as many photos as we wished.

"Can we recreate the crime scene photos?" I asked our guide. I had seen them hundreds of times in my collection of Lizzie Borden books, and they were also framed and placed in the two murder rooms.

"Of course," he said and smiled.

I took the photo of Andrew Borden off the fireplace mantel and showed it to my husband so he could position himself reclined on the black leather divan in the parlor. This was how Lizzie's father, Andrew Borden, was found with his skull mutilated.

Then the three of us went upstairs to the bedroom where Lizzie's stepmother was murdered. I looked at her photograph on the bureau, then got down on my hands and knees and posed facedown on the floor by the bed where Abby was found. Not my better side. I felt for Abby, a rather large woman, being discovered with her knees slightly bent so her rump was her distinguishing feature.

Lizzie's room was furnished with antiques of the period when the murders occurred, 1892, as well as several portrait photographs of her. The double bed had a white eyelet duvet and matching white sheets with an eyelet trim. Two chairs and a round tea table were placed in the room's corner. The bathroom was across the hall. I'm not sure where our host went after we retired to Lizzie's room, but as I recall, legally, he had to stay on the premises when guests occupied the house.

Oh, how I was scared and excited and nervous and as thrilled as a child standing on the platform in anticipation of boarding the Banshee roller coaster, primed for any and all paranormal activity when we turned off the lights. I lay awake, heart rapping in my chest and eyes straining wildly in the dark, expecting something to happen. Surely I'd hear noises, see apparitions, or feel an icy ghostly hand touch my cheek. Sleep finally overcame me, and I awoke to sunlight streaming through the window. For what we paid, you'd think the damn host could have at least floated around with a white sheet over his head, moaning and rattling a chain or something. The whole stay was disappointingly uneventful.

Even though it embarrassed me to admit I suffered from PD (psychical dysfunction) when I visited Lizzie Borden's house all those years ago, surely my Catholic upbringing wasn't all for naught in my quest to become a medium in my mid-fifties. Catholics are brought up with a reverence for spirits. The Catholic Mass itself is a morphing of pagan rituals, with its altar, symbolic sacrificial consumption of the body and blood of Christ, and candle and incense burning. Catholics offer Masses, light candles, and say prayers for the deceased's soul. They celebrate All Souls' Day on November 2. They pray to saints—once humans, now spirits who make appearances on occasion. (You aren't supposed to communicate with the unsainted dead, though.) They believe in the resurrection of the dead via the physical body's spirit. They believe in a Holy Ghost or Holy Spirit. Children are taught that they are protected by guardian angels. And priests not only have the ability to perform baptisms, marriages, and last rites for the soul, but some are trained in exorcising evil spirits.

But as a fifty-six-year-old woman, where would I start in learning how to become a medium? If I couldn't conjure the dead in my teens, would it be any different now? Salt Lake City, Utah, was great for genealogy, but not exactly the capital of mediumship. Mormons, who predominate here, believe in a spirit world and in spirit visitations from their loved ones. They just don't talk about that with "outsiders." Only their upper-echelon leaders are supposed to be in direct communication with God.

I searched online for mediumship development classes in my area. Nothing. I searched online for mediums who might take me under their wing. A few came up but none resonated with me. They all believed in God, saying it was a gift from God. When you don't believe in a so-called God, how can you get the gift? Were there gift cards I could purchase on Amazon perhaps? Then I discovered *correspondence courses* on becoming a medium. I wouldn't even have to leave home. The spirits would come to me.

The Morris Pratt Institute, founded in 1899 in Milwaukee, Wisconsin, offered distance-learning courses in becoming a Spiritualist minister, a Spiritualist healer, a Spiritualist teacher, and a Spiritualist medium. Their program, endorsed and recommended by the National Spiritualist Association of Churches, would prepare me to be a certified Spiritualist medium. There was only one problem. After taking the courses, I would have to be a member of (and attend regularly) one of their churches to become certified. I searched their directory. That wouldn't be easy. The nearest church was either in Las Vegas or Reno, Nevada.

So, I turned to books. The first book I found looked made-to-order: *So You Want to Be a Medium?* by Spiritualist minister Rose Vanden Eynden. In it, she claimed that everyone has the ability to become a medium—good, so far—but to develop that ability, I'd have to *meditate*. Daily. That part didn't excite me. As was the case when I didn't like what someone told me, I looked for a second opinion. Or a third. And maybe a fourth, until I found what *I* wanted to hear. But each of the three other books I read on communicating with spirits, all also written by Spiritualist ministers, said the same thing. Daily meditation was key to spirit communication. It's while your mind is quiet that spirits can slip in and tell you what's on their minds. One author said that it was best to meditate in the evening, as spirits are more active then. What? They get to sleep in? I would enjoy being a spirit one day.

One author suggested meditating at 8 p.m. for a couple of reasons. First, you didn't want to meditate on a full stomach, as the noises generated by your digestive juices might prove distracting. Plus, on a full stomach, you're more likely to fall asleep. That made sense. Second, she too said the spirits are move active in the evening. This raised another dilemma not covered in any of the books: 8 p.m. in which time zone? I didn't want to miss the spirits if I meditated too early or too late. And how do you know what time zone they're coming from?

The authors insisted that meditation at the same time every day was important. As certified medium and Spiritualist minister Elizabeth Owens put it in *How to Communicate with Spirits*, you were "keeping a date with Spirit." It was no different than keeping a lunch date with a friend. If you continually canceled that date or didn't show up, your friend wasn't going to bother either. I guess spirits were busy and kept to a schedule, too.

My life was already full with teaching online college writing classes and researching and writing family history books for clients. How was I going to work in a daily meditation, even for the ten minutes the books agreed was the minimum? I'd done some yoga meditation in the past and meditated for maybe a minute and twenty-two seconds, but ten? I'd also done some reading about Zen Buddhism. The idea of being mindful, calming my "monkey mind," and living in the present had appealed to me when I read about it a few years prior, but the discipline it required went against everything I'd lived by for the past half century. I'd refined the habit of replaying past mistakes and worrying about the future. Who had time to add living in the present to all that? To begin a daily meditation schedule to communicate with spirits sounded like it would mean a total rewiring of my brain and my life. Just how badly did I want to talk to the dead? Was it even possible for me to sit still for ten minutes without the TV on or a book in my hands?

Likewise, doing anything at 8 p.m. would be a challenge for me. That's an hour before I prepared for bed, and there was good TV on then. Although Jim wasn't interested in trying to become a medium, he was game to try meditating with me. Who couldn't use a little peace and tranquility in their life? So, after a lengthy discussion spanning several days of debating potentially good times to meditate and why they wouldn't work, we settled on 8 p.m.—Eastern time, which was 6 p.m. Mountain time where we lived. This would be before I made dinner and right after we watched the nightly national news. We could use a little calming meditation after that.

Meditation is critical to spirit communication, explained the books, because spirit energy exists at a faster vibration rate, while we mere mortals occupy a lower vibration rate. All energy vibrates, some more so than others. A tree trunk has a lower vibration energy than a hummingbird. Even though spirits might be around us, we can't see them because of their high vibration. Think of it like looking at a helicopter's rotor blades. When the helicopter isn't moving, you can see the blades, but when the pilot starts the engine and the blades engage, you can't see the blades anymore, just as you can't make out the wings of a hummingbird in flight.

Spirits are the same way. We might get a glimpse of them out of the corner of an eye, but when you turn to look, there's nothing there. That's spirit energy. Your eye caught this higher vibration for a split second. When we meditate, it allows us to calm our busy minds, freeing us from the visual and emotional clutter of daily life. Meditation also utilizes a different part of the brain than daydreaming or cognitive activities. This tranquil state raises our own energy vibrations. When spirits see we are open to communicating with them, they lower their vibration level so we can meet halfway. Or so the books said.

Many of the meditation exercises I read about encouraged envisioning the peacefulness of nature by mentally imagining a stroll along the beach or a hike in the mountains. Right. I wasn't a fan of the outdoors. I understood the "one with nature" bit, but I'd no sooner hike in the mountains—all those bugs—than I would walk on the beach—all that sand.

I loved the small yard of our condo, though. The year we moved in, we planted a blaze maple tree in one corner that now shaded the patio from the morning sun, and a weeping cherry tree as the yard's center focal point. Around the fence, we planted lilacs (that never flowered), rose of Sharon bushes, hollyhocks, plus other various flowering plants that attracted bees and damselflies. A patch of catnip kept our black-and-white kitty Figaro happy. We'd hung bird feeders, and one summer, we had a garden water fountain under our living room window. The three tiers provided a soothing, relaxing trickle both when we were outside and inside with the window open. But our hard water quickly calcified and clogged the pump, so it became just an ornament. We spent summer mornings enjoying tea on the patio, listening to the screech of seagulls (we're not far from the Great Salt Lake), the coo of mourning doves, and the chirp of crickets; in the late afternoon, I relished my time on the patio to read and sip a glass of chilled Riesling. I assumed when I meditated I could substitute this scene for the sand, shell shards, bugs, and bears.

The books said that during meditation, the first thing you should strive to see with your "third eye" is colors. Some believe the third eye is the pineal gland, located in the brain behind the third cerebral ventricle, midline between the two hemispheres of the brain. That is, it's aligned with the middle of your forehead, close to the eyebrows, where South and Southeast Asian women wear a bindi, or jewel. The pineal gland, named because it resembles the shape of a pine cone, is the endocrine gland that produces melatonin, which is responsible for a good night's sleep. The gland is larger in children, which is why they sleep so soundly, and it shrinks and can become calcified as we age, which is why older folks don't sleep as well. Wonderful. At my age, I had to work with not only a hardened but probably a cataracted third eye. Was there Lasik surgery for that?

French philosopher René Descartes (1596–1650) believed that the pineal gland was the seat of the soul and connected the body with the intellect. Some Eastern religious philosophies, such as Hinduism and Buddhism, believe that this gland, the third eye, is related to the ajna chakra, which allows a person to achieve higher states of consciousness and to develop clairvoyant perception. Since everyone has a pineal gland, it's believed this is the reason everyone has some degree of psychic ability or intuition.

Chakras are seven specific areas of the body that produce life forces, a.k.a. "energies." These chakras also produce spectra of light. The third-eye chakra was associated with the color indigo. Because we're inundated with visual media, from televisions to computers, these images clutter the vision of our third eye. One way to clear away all that visual junk is to meditate, thereby activating and raising the vibration level of the pineal gland and thus clairvoyant abilities.

Before Jim and I had set our "date with Spirit," I decided to try a preview meditation one night before falling asleep. With the room blackened, I shut my eyes and tried to visualize colors. It was a lot harder than I thought! You weren't drawing from memory; you're actually trying to see a color. All I saw was black. After a few minutes, I saw a darting flash of purple. Then blackness again. At one point, I saw white light that looked like an open hallway. *Uh-oh*, I thought. This can't be good. So, I ended my meditation session and went to sleep. When I later shared the flashes of color and white-light experience with my daughter, Laurie, she said, "You were probably having a stroke."

CHAPTER 4

Signs, Skeptics, and Science

My genealogy friend and colleague Dwight—who asked that I describe him as, ahem, tall, dark, and handsome—and I traveled for a second time to Ireland for our client. This was a few years before I decided to become a medium and two months after Jim and I began our relationship. Dwight had done the Irish genealogical research on the client's ancestry, and he'd been to Ireland many times. When the client wanted his family history written, Dwight had recommended me. I started drafting the family history after our first trip in the spring of 2002, but eighteen months later, I could see where I still had holes in the life stories of the client's ancestors.

We revisited many of the places we'd been to before—off-the-beaten-path ancestral homesites, cottage ruins, and cemeteries—but we now interviewed people and visited different museums and folk parks so I could get more of a sense of the history of Ireland and Irish life in the nineteenth century. As we drove by a road sign that gave the mileage to Knock, in County Mayo in the west of Ireland, Dwight said, "Oh! We need to go there. You'll really like Knock."

Knock was where the Virgin Mary was said to have made a guest appearance in 1879 in the south gable of Knock Parish Church. Fifteen people witnessed the apparition, and a shrine to the Blessed Virgin stands there today. We had not planned this stop, but we weren't in a hurry that day, and we both loved gift shops. Knock had plenty.

We walked into the first shop, and I had never seen so many religious statues in as many shapes and sizes in all my life. Along with plastic and painted plaster of Paris saints, the usual Irish souvenir "shit-shop" items made in China stacked the shelves, from T-shirts to mugs, most with Mary's heavenly face beaming on them. Dwight went off to find a restroom while I browsed. I came to a rack filled with prayer trading cards sporting images of what seemed like every saint ever canonized. My eye was drawn to a card for St. Clare.

Clare was Jim's mother's name; she had died six years earlier. Picking up the card, I read the prayer on the back. Then I heard in my mind, "Buy this for Jimmy." I'd never called him "Jimmy" during the two months I'd been dating him. Even as goofy as I thought it sounded, I felt as if it were his mother telling me to buy the card. I purchased it, then found Dwight. We visited the shrine and wandered through at least a half dozen more shops. At each one, I looked at the racks of saints' cards. None of the others carried one for St. Clare.

Back home, a week later, Jim and I dined at Carrabba's, my favorite Italian restaurant, after I had picked him up from the airport. He had been in St. Paul, Minnesota, his hometown, while I'd been in Ireland. Like any couple newly in love, we conversed in the chatter of romantics.

Over my chicken marsala and fettuccini alfredo, I told him, "I know what you do for me to make me feel loved and secure, but I can't see what I do for you. Why do you love me so much?"

The moment I verbalized the question, a thought, which I can only describe as not my own, came into my head: *You're giving him his life back.*

I almost didn't say anything because it sounded rather egotistical, but then I thought, *No, I need to tell him this. It's important. Clare wants me to tell him this.*

Before Jim could answer me, I said, "Wait! Clare just told me that I'm giving you your life back."

Jim nearly spit out his Coke. He went white and looked as if he had seen, well, a ghost. He sat across from me speechless. The hum of the other diners filtered in my ears like white noise.

"What?" I asked. "What did I say?"

He found his voice and said, "Right before I flew out here, I stopped at the cemetery on my way to the airport to visit my parents' graves. I talked to my mom, and I thanked her for leading me to you and *giving me my life back*."

Now I was speechless. And riddled with goose bumps.

"I even wrote it down," he said and pulled from his back pants' pocket a three-by-five note card to show me. "Although I wasn't sure *why* I wrote it down."

When we started dating, Jim called me Rose. He gave me a copy of *The Little Prince* by Antoine de Saint-Exupéry. In it, he included a note that said, "Read this. Then you'll understand why I call you Rose." Sometimes I'm not very bright. I didn't understand the connection with the nickname. I told him I didn't get it.

"Keep reading," he said.

This was when Jim learned I was not a patient person and all about the destination. I came to chapter twenty-one, where the fox explains to the Little Prince that even though there are thousands of roses, the Little Prince's rose is unique and special, because she is the one he loves. "But my rose, all on her own, is more important than all of you together. . . . Since she's *my* rose," I read. Aw. How could I not be enamored with Jim even more? Plus, my Irish grandmother's name was Rose, which he had no way of knowing.

Some nine months later, on our first trip to Ireland together, I wanted to show Jim the gift shop in Knock where his mother nudged me to buy the St. Clare prayer card. I remembered it as the first one in the row of shops, but when we entered and I looked around, it didn't look as familiar as in my memory.

"Let's try the next one," I said. As soon as we entered it, I knew this wasn't the right place and turned around. "No, it's the one we were just in."

We returned just seconds later, and lying on the floor in the middle of the entryway was a cellophane-wrapped pin on a cardboard holder. The pin was a single red rose with a gold stem. We both stopped and stared at it. I turned to Jim. "That wasn't there before, was it?"

Jim was as wide eyed as I was.

"No, it wasn't."

I picked it up. "She's here."

"I guess we'd better buy the pin." Jim grinned.

Strange things kept happening to me after I started seeing Jim in my late forties, before I'd made the decision to intentionally become a medium. It never entered my mind that these events had anything to do with being a medium. After all, many people experience signs like this from a loved one who's passed. I assumed his mom wanted us to know she was giving us her blessing.

Each time I shared these experiences with Laurie, though, she'd either humor me or say, "It was just a coincidence." If you couldn't tell, my daughter doesn't believe in spirits or anything paranormal, let alone God or Jesus. Those Bible study classes didn't make an impression on her, which was fine with me. Although we never discussed religion or the afterlife, we both lived an agnostic existence. My mini-me in most things—we shared the same hour-glass figure, most definitely the same hips, and the same timbre to our voices. If you were to ask me how

I'd describe Laurie in three words or less, I'd say intelligent, funny, and open minded. But apparently not about this. She is a scientist, a biology and anatomy high school teacher. As such, she wanted me to find scientific evidence that spirits exist. I didn't blame her. Some solid evidence would be good for me, too, not just for my peace of mind, but to show Laurie that her mother wasn't entirely a delusional freak.

What I really looked for was the science that would convince Laurie. I knew where mainstream, materialistic science stood. They called all this weird stuff "pseudoscience," not the real deal. Mainstream science offered logical explanations, even though sometimes there weren't any. They believed that visions were hallucinations, near-death experiences were biochemical reactions in the brain as it shut down, and voices in your head meant, well, maybe it's time to see a psychiatrist. But I didn't see it that way. Was I biased? You bet. Were they? You bet. But as David Fontana, PhD, wrote in his article "Disbelief Despite the Evidence," "A cardinal rule in science is that you familiarize yourself with the evidence before making judgments on it." That's what I hoped my skeptic daughter would do. I wanted her to understand my point of view and what I was discovering.

The word *skeptic* comes from the Greek *skeptikos*, meaning "inquiring, reflective," which I considered myself. In the early 1600s, an extended definition was added: "one with a doubting attitude." According to one online dictionary, a skeptic is "a person who questions or doubts something (such as a claim or statement): a person who often questions or doubts things." I've discovered that some people who call themselves skeptics are not questioners, nor are they open minded toward investigating the scientific research into unexplained phenomena. They are what some call *pseudoskeptics*, people who have reached their opinions not after careful research and examination of the paranormal scientific literature but based on secondhand knowledge, ingrained preconceptions, or a refusal to be honestly open to evaluating the evidence.

Laurie, like many others with science backgrounds, believes that when you die, that's it. There is no afterlife. You just cease to exist.

The first law of thermodynamics, though, says that energy cannot be created or destroyed; it can only be transformed. Those who believe in an afterlife say that the energy from our personalities, our souls, our consciousnesses, transforms into an energy called "spirit" and continues to survive after we die. And, come to find out, there existed a decent body of controlled scientific experiments that appeared to support this. As Harvard psychologist and paranormal researcher Dr. William James (1842–1910) once said, "In order to disprove the law that all crows are black, it is enough to find one white crow."

One problem with testing those in the spirit world is that they are former humans; they are predictably unpredictable. Or, as Dr. Dean Radin says in *Entangled Minds: Extrasensory Experiences in a Quantum Reality*, "Hardly anything involving skilled human performance is absolutely predictable, except perhaps stubbornness in the face of evidence one doesn't wish to see." When doing any kind of experiments with humans, this anomaly has to be factored in. Just as you and I today have free will, it makes sense that we'd have that same free will in an afterlife. Spirit people wouldn't be like a dog that comes on command. Spirit people would be more like cats. If they feel like communicating, they will. If they don't, they won't.

Many who believe in an afterlife say that when we depart this life, we take our personalities, along with our opinions, knowledge, and beliefs that we held in life. If, while alive, a person didn't believe that spirit communication was possible, he might not be inclined to try communicating after he's dead. Or to wake up in the afterlife and "see the light." Others might not be able to communicate for one reason or another. They may be doing a life review and healing and not ready to deal with issues from while they were on earth. But no one is ever "stuck" between worlds. You're either in the physical world or the spirit world. Some may choose to stay close to the earth plane, but they are not "stuck" or "lost."

As I learned, mediums receive information through all of their senses. A medium might see images in her mind's eye; hear words, music, or voices in her mind's ear; smell scents; taste foods; or feel the symptoms of ailments or experience the departed's cause of death. These are phenomena referred to as the "clairs." The clairs correspond to our physical senses—sight, sound, taste, touch, smell—but we experience them on another level. Clairvoyance is for clear seeing in the mind's eye, clairaudience for clear hearing in the mind's ear, and so forth.

Mediums have no control over which spirit might come through, during a reading or which clairs they might trigger in their communication. But when a spirit is present, the medium must be able to discern the spirit's message from her own thoughts, as well as translate the message she's receiving. The medium might receive a message about which she has no personal frame of reference. Say she's hearing a foreign word or phrase, for example. She wouldn't be able to understand what she's getting, in which case her own consciousness may filter it out.

If a medium gets something wrong, that doesn't necessarily mean she's a fraud. No medium is 100 percent accurate; neither are doctors, lawyers, ministers, scientists, writers, or any other human being. A medium could misinterpret the message she's received. This is why mediums typically ask the sitter for confirmation, so they know they've made a connection with the loved one in spirit.

Scientists are tidy people. They like things that they can replicate in a controlled laboratory setting. I found plenty of peer-reviewed articles with experiments that dealt with psychic abilities, but the studies that most interested me were the ones to determine whether consciousness survives physical death and, if so, whether our afterlife consciousness can communicate with the living. Lo and behold, I found a number of lab-based, controlled studies involving "research mediums" that attempted to answer these same questions. Published in peer-reviewed journals written primarily by physicists and psychologists, these experiments dealt with the accuracy and replicability of "anomalous information" (that is, after-death communication and telepathy).

Experiments conducted independently by researchers in the United States and the United Kingdom used highly controlled double-, triple-, and even quintuple-blind protocols with these research mediums.

Bear with me, okay? I know this next part gets complicated. For example, here are the objectives and protocols as explained in one article, "A Double-Blind Procedure for Assessing the Relevance of a Medium's Statements to a Recipient" by Archie E. Roy, Department of Physics and Astronomy at Glasgow University, and Tricia J. Robertson, Scottish Society for Psychical Research:

> To assess the ability of a *medium* to make relevant statements with respect to a *recipient* when:—
>
> a.) the medium and recipient are hidden from each other's view;
> b.) the recipient does not speak to the medium;
> c.) the recipient does not know he [or she] is the recipient;
> d.) the medium cannot identify the recipient in any normal way;
> e.) each of the other participants is unaware of whether he [or she] is the recipient or a *non-recipient*;
> f.) neither of the two investigators chooses the recipient.

Robertson and Roy conducted a two-year study involving 10 mediums, 44 recipients, and 407 non-recipients. They concluded that "there was a highly significant difference between the fractions of statements accepted by the non-recipients and by the recipients . . . . This ostensibly falsified the hypothesis that the statements made by mediums to recipients are so general that they could be accepted by anyone. . . . The recipients accepted a higher proportion of statements from mediums as relevant to their lives than did non-recipients." The mediums, they concluded, demonstrated that they acquired information in a paranormal way.

The mediums involved in these studies had not only a reputation for being legitimate, with a high accuracy rate, but passed a rigorous screening process for the studies, which included personality and psychological tests, several interviews, and at least two blind readings.

For studies conducted at the University of Arizona, Dr. Gary E. Schwartz (PhD from Harvard and a former professor of psychology and psychiatry at Yale University, in case you wondered) developed similar certification criteria. Those mediums who passed the screening were considered certified research mediums. In 2017, the Windbridge Institute for Applied Research in Human Potential, located in Tucson, Arizona, and now called the Windbridge Research Center, continued this screening process and certification, as well as testing.

Double-blind, and even triple-blind, mediumship studies conducted by Dr. Schwartz and his colleagues reached conclusions similar to Robertson and Roy's studies. Dr. Schwartz explained the complex, elaborate protocol and provided case studies in his book, *The Truth about* Medium: *Extraordinary Experiments with the Real Allison DuBois of NBC's* Medium *and Other Remarkable Psychics*. (Many of these studies appeared in peer-reviewed journals.) The certified research mediums were told and reminded before each experiment, in a nutshell, that if they were ever caught cheating, they would be publicly exposed as frauds. The same warning was issued to all those who participated in the experiments, from sitters to staff.

In the double-blind studies, the medium wasn't told for whom she'd be doing the reading (the majority of research mediums are women) or the name of the deceased whom the sitter wanted to contact. Likewise, the sitter wasn't told who the medium was. In fact, neither medium nor sitter were together in the same proximity. At a designated time, the sitter was instructed to think of their loved one from whom they wanted to receive a message. A proxy sitter then asked the medium questions, such as "What does the discarnate [spirit person] look like?" "Describe the discarnate's personality." "What hobbies or activities did the discarnate like to do?" "What was the discarnate's cause of death?"

Transcripts were made of the audio digital files. The sitter, however, was sent two different written transcriptions of readings to review and rate, one from the medium involved in the experiment and one reading that had been prepared for someone else. The sitter then scored the information on both for accuracy.

In a triple-blind study, not only did the medium and sitter have no contact, but the research assistant who served as the proxy sitter was blind to the identities of the medium, the sitter, and the deceased loved one. The medium would have no visual or auditory clues, positive or negative, from the proxy sitter, as he or she didn't know any information to confirm or deny. Likewise, because the proxy sitter was clueless, it eliminated the possibility that the medium read relevant clues from the proxy sitter's mind. Even Dr. Schwartz was constantly amazed by the successful results these experiments produced. The sitters overwhelmingly picked, beyond the statistics of chance, which reading was theirs.

In one of Dr. Schwartz's double-blind experiments, the medium lived in Connecticut and the two sitters resided in Europe. One of his goals, though, was to determine whether mediums received telepathic messages from the living person, or if they were indeed communicating with the dead. Since, in this particular experiment, he knew the medium, the European sitters, and with whom the sitters wanted to communicate (a deceased famous person one of the sitters knew), the medium could have read Dr. Schwartz's mind. Based on the medium's reading, however, it became clear this wasn't the case. The medium could not identify the famous person by name, as the celebrity wouldn't show her face. But the medium could describe the famous person's physical appearance (height, build, hair color, and dress), characteristics, personal life details, and cause of death, which were all correct.

Additionally, in some of Dr. Schwartz's experiments, his own deceased mother and a now-deceased medium with whom he had once worked "dropped in." As Dr. Schwartz says, "Survival is in the details." These deceased women communicated to the mediums, providing details only Dr. Schwartz and his mother, or he and the deceased medium, could have known. He writes in *The Truth About* Medium (the name of a TV series at the time), "When the artificiality of the laboratory replicates real-life phenomena for a given medium, it logically follows that we should treat the real-life phenomena for that medium as genuine."

Dr. Julie Beischel, co-founder and director of research for the Windbridge Institute for Applied Research in Human Potential, and her colleagues devised a quintuple-blind protocol. She described it in minute detail in her thirty-two-page article, "Contemporary Methods in Laboratory-Based Mediumship Research." I won't go into the rather complicated details. (You can Google the title and find it, if you're interested.) Suffice it to say that the protocol was so elaborate that, as Beischel says in her article, "This entire scenario eliminates fraud, cold-reading, rater bias, experimenter cuing, and perhaps even telepathy of the experimenter and/or absent sitter as plausible explanations for the accuracy and specificity of the information provided during readings."

Legitimate scientists, regardless of their personal beliefs (and many paranormal researchers admit they are agnostic), are obligated to follow the research findings wherever they lead, and to report negative as well as positive findings. They do not relegate the failed research to the "file drawer." The authors of the articles I've studied on mediumship research were up front about "misses" as well as "hits," and they objectively analyzed the information the medium provided. The blinded mediumship studies conducted by Drs. Schwartz, Beischel, Roy, Robertson, and their colleagues reached the same conclusion, as Dr. Beischel and Adam J. Rock summarized in "Addressing the Survival Versus Psi Debate through Process-Focused Mediumship Research":

Skilled mediums are able to report information that is both accurate and specific about the deceased loved ones (termed discarnates) of living people (termed sitters) using anomalous information reception . . . without any prior knowledge about the discarnates or sitters, in the absence of any sensory feedback, and without using deceptive means.

Oh, dear. Did I just see a flock of white crows flying overhead?

While looking for scientific literature, I discovered that respected institutions such as Princeton University, the University of Arizona, the University of Virginia Medical School, the University of Amsterdam, the University of Edinburgh, and the University of Hertfordshire in England, to name a few, have entire departments with ongoing programs in paranormal studies. There are also several independent labs, such as the Windbridge Institute, the Institute of Noetic Sciences, and the Rhine Research Center (formerly affiliated with Duke University), that conduct paranormal research experiments. Some prefer to use the less mystical-sounding term of "consciousness studies," but these studies join together the disciplines of neuroscience, physics, and psychology. There still exists, too, the Parapsychological Association. Since 1969, it has continued to be an affiliate of the American Association for the Advancement of Science, the world's largest scientific society.

My English composition students often ask me how much research is enough for a paper topic. I tell them that when the sources start to sound redundant, you've probably done enough research. Short of reading some six hundred or so additional books and hundreds of other articles on consciousness survival, I'd done enough research to be convinced that there is sound, legitimate scientific evidence for mediumship abilities and the survival of consciousness. But was it enough to convince Laurie?

"I've done the research you asked about." I was excited to call Laurie and tell her.

"What?" She had obviously forgotten the task she'd given me of finding scientific journal articles.

"The scientific research with studies that show consciousness survives physical death," I said.

Silence.

"I'd like to email you the articles."

More silence.

"Oh. That's okay," she said.

It frustrated me that Laurie refused to look at the scientific evidence once I discovered it. I understood that this exploration was my journey, not hers. That it was now my passionate interest, but not hers. That life and an afterlife look different in your mid-to-late fifties than your early thirties.

I realized, too, that it was about more than trying to convince her there was an afterlife. I sought her approval. I wanted her to be as proud of me as I was of her and her accomplishments in her career as a science teacher. I had no doubt she was proud of me and my genealogy career as a national speaker and writer, but now? Would she carry that same acceptance and pride if I were to become a medium? Or would she be embarrassed by me?

In the delivery room that Labor Day weekend long ago, when the doctor announced, "It's a girl," I swore she and I would not have the same troubled mother-daughter relationship I'd had with my mother. Sandwiched then between my daughter and my mother, I instinctively chose Laurie. I gave all my attention and energy to form a bond with her, leaving little for my mother.

From the moment Laurie could talk, she and I spoke about everything. We had always been close and like-minded. Sure, we'd had our moments of mother-daughter angst, when she'd storm out of the house. She always frustrated easily. One day, her hair wasn't cooperating. I heard her stomping and yelling in the upstairs bathroom. When she came downstairs, I sat at the kitchen table reading and, without looking up, I couldn't resist saying, "Did you *want* your hair to look that way?"

"Aargh!" The windows rattled when she slammed the door.

When Laurie went off to college, she'd call home once, twice, three times a day. The separation anxiety, wailing, and keening seemed endless, but then Laurie would calm me down, and I enjoyed listening to her tales about her new life in the dorm and her classes. When she was in high school, her career goal had been to sing on Broadway. She attended show-choir camps and performed onstage. She also participated in state singing competitions. But she didn't make the cut for the university choir. That's when science classes grabbed her interest, and I ended up getting the blame for telling her in high school she'd never use algebra.

The summer after she graduated high school, Laurie and I traveled to New York City to sightsee. A friend of mine on Long Island rode the train into Manhattan every day with one of the cameramen for the soap opera *One Life to Live*, which Laurie watched with me during summer breaks. He arranged for us to visit the studio, meet some of the actors during their rehearsal, and see how the show was filmed. When Laurie left for college, she'd sometimes call during her lunch break, and we'd watch the show together over the phone, commenting on characters and storylines, reminiscing about our trip to the studio.

One of my treasured memories occurred when we went to Italy together in her junior year of high school with a friend of mine and her daughter. We stayed a few days in Potenza in Southern Italy, my friend's ancestral town. While they attended an evening Mass in the ancestral church, Laurie and I strolled the main thoroughfare with the rest of Potenza. In this traditional evening pastime, men and women promenaded arm in arm, but so did teenage girls, old men, and mothers and daughters. I can't recall whether I looped my arm in Laurie's or she looped hers in mine, but when in Potenza . . . We shared an intimate moment that I hadn't experienced since breastfeeding her. I cherished it more, actually. She willingly hooked arms with me. This wasn't an infant's instinct for nourishment. It was a conscious choice. We walked, chatted, and browsed in storefronts until our feet ached.

But now, she's grown and feeling more like a stranger. She'd changed, and I was changing. It terrified me that we would grow apart, that I would lose her in my aspiration to give new purpose to my life. She wasn't taking my mediumship seriously. And worse, what would happen when I die? She wouldn't acknowledge me when I try to communicate with her from the spirit world. When she hears me calling her name, she'll think she's hearing things. When I move her toothbrush to the other side of the bathroom counter, she'll think she unconsciously did it. When she feels that cool air on her cheek where I'm kissing her goodnight and sending thoughts of "I love you, Pooh Bear," she'll think there's a draft. When she thinks of me and wishes I were there for some turning point in her life—even though I will be— she might wish she could believe, but her material science won't let her.

I realized something else. When someone has held a belief in something for a long time, whether it be science, religion, or a belief or disbelief in an afterlife, the thought that this belief might not be accurate is daunting and threatening. Fundamental theories of material science that she and my son-in-law, a high school physics teacher, have studied, accepted, and now teach would be in jeopardy. Medium-based research poses a threat to much in the currently held scientific status quo, just as quantum theory upsets the foundation of classical physics.

What would happen if Laurie and her husband studied and debated those articles on mediumship I'd found and came to accept, at least as possible, that the research on consciousness survival was valid. Where would this leave them as science teachers? Perhaps open to the same doubt and sneers I now faced from skeptics, including possibly jeopardizing their jobs and the respect of their colleagues. Worse yet, what if Laurie became convinced, but her husband remained a skeptic? What strife might this bring to their marriage?

As much as I wanted my daughter to be likewise convinced by the scientific evidence I'd found, the stakes might be too high for her to shift away from her known and accepted truth. I get that. The stakes were already high for me. Was I unintentionally putting a rift in my relationship with her? If so, was I willing to give up on this quest?

CHAPTER 5

My Mother the Spirit

I didn't make it in time to see my mother one last time before she died in the nursing home in Colorado. When I had called her that Mother's Day in 2011, she sounded frail and weak. I talked with the nurse on duty, and she told me Mom hadn't been eating. The next morning, Peggy, the head nurse, called and said to come. "We'll be there tomorrow," I told her, then I signed and faxed papers for palliative care.

I napped in the van while Jim drove the twelve hours to our destination from Salt Lake City. Peggy called my cell phone around one o'clock while we were partway through barren Wyoming to say Mom's breathing grew heavier. She wasn't sure we'd make it in time. She said a staff member had been with Mom all day, telling her to hang on, that I was on the way. A little after three, Peggy called again. "She's gone." I couldn't speak. Sobs overcame me, my heart as desolate as the scenery blurring by the window. I handed the phone to Jim.

Brenda, the nursing home director, had been the last to sit with Mom. She read her Bible verses, sang hymns, and talked to her. Brenda told my mom that she hadn't been able to be with her dad or her mother-in-law when they passed, and she would be honored to be there for her. She told my mom again that I was on the way, but said if she couldn't hold on, Brenda knew that I would understand. Ten minutes later, my mother passed.

When I saw the flower arrangements for the memorial service that Friday, I looked at the one with the white carnations and lilies my cousin had sent. Lilies are traditional for funerals and memorial services because they symbolize the soul's resurrection. Five of the lilies had bloomed, but one large blossom had yet to open. I wondered whether cut lilies still bloom.

After the memorial service, Jim suggested I donate the flowers to the nursing home, but I wanted to take them back to the hotel room. I set the lily arrangement on top of the TV so I'd see whether or not the large lily would open.

We planned to head back to Utah on Sunday. On Saturday afternoon, we stopped at a store to pick up a few items for the road. Our van, which had been operating fine until now, developed a grinding noise when Jim put the transmission in reverse. He turned off the ignition, and we sat in the van while he pondered the problem and our options. He called a nearby transmission shop, but they were already closed. We decided to rent a car and leave the van at the transmission place for when they opened Monday morning. Before we called AAA to tow the van, then a cab to take us for a rental car, Jim started the ignition once more and tried putting it into gear again. It worked fine. We discussed attempting the long drive back home tomorrow but knew we should get the transmission checked. We drove the van to the car rental place, then to the transmission shop without incident.

We arrived when the shop opened on Monday, where the smell of grease and oil hung heavily in the air. Jim explained what had happened. The mechanic, in his navy shirt with a patch sewn over the pocket telling us his name was Joe, said he'd look it over and call us. An hour later, Joe said that on the test drive, he hadn't felt or heard anything, but when he dropped the transmission pan, it brimmed with gunk and metal shavings—the worst he'd ever seen for a vehicle that showed no symptoms and was still drivable. Joe marveled that we had made it not only from Utah but had driven around in the four days since we had arrived. Each day, we drove over a hundred miles as we commuted between Colorado Springs and the nursing home in Simla.

I hadn't started my mediumship journey yet, but my Catholic upbringing convinced me someone watched over us. Maybe my mother had reincarnated into the van and would talk to me through the car's transmission, as Jerry Van Dyke's TV mom did through the radio in *My Mother the Car*. Come to think of it, the grinding noise did sound like my mother's voice at times.

One thing's certain—had we not had that hint of trouble in the parking lot, we would have headed home the next day. Given what the mechanic said, we would have broken down in the Middle-of-Nowhere-Without-Cell-Phone-Reception, Wyoming.

The funeral home kept my mother on ice. Her doctor had left town, and the funeral home wouldn't transport Mom to Denver for cremation until the doctor signed the death certificate. A week to the day that she died, the funeral home called to say that Mom had finally been cremated. Still in Colorado waiting on the van repairs, I looked at the lily flower arrangement on top of the television in our hotel room. The bud, which had been unopened last night, was in full bloom.

With the van fixed, we headed home. The funeral home was seventy-five miles in the opposite direction, so I asked them to ship Mom's cremains to us.

Not ready to part with the flower arrangement, which still looked good, I brought it home. Over the days after our return, the large lily gradually lost one petal at a time.

By Friday, my mother hadn't shown up yet. I called the funeral home the following Monday, and they confirmed that the cremains had been shipped.

Mom finally arrived ten days after she'd been cremated. The last petal on the lily fell off that same day.

My birthday that October was bittersweet. This would be my first birthday without her. I didn't think it would bother me too much because not only was our relationship turbulent, but in her later years, half the time she didn't remember which day was my birthday. One year she called to wish me a happy birthday on my daughter's birthday, saying, "Well, I knew it was somebody's birthday."

But as my day approached, I realized this would be the first year, too, that I wouldn't hear those treasured words from my mother's lips: "Take a few dollars out of my checking account and buy yourself a birthday gift." Of course, she resided in a nursing home, so it wasn't as if she could go shopping, nor could she write checks because I had her checkbook to pay her bills. Because she survived off fifty dollars a month after I paid her bills, I never took more than about fifteen dollars and usually bought myself a book.

Two days before my birthday, the mail brought a package from Brenda, the nursing home director. Inside was a note taped around a small, green change purse:

Sharon & Jim,

Hope all is well with you. I found this in my file. I totally forgot that your mom had given it to me for safe keeping. It's not much but it was important to her. We think of her often. She is still in our hearts.

Brenda

Inside the change purse, I found thirteen dollars and some change.

When I emailed Brenda to let her know the change purse had not only arrived but in time for my birthday, I asked her if she had known it was my birthday. She didn't.

But my mom knew, and she'd remembered correctly this year.

Some (Laurie) would say that the timing of the lily bud's bloom and demise, the forewarning of the transmission problems, and the arrival of my mom's change purse in time for my birthday were nothing more than coincidence. If only one of these events had happened, perhaps I would have agreed. I guess it boils down to whether you believe in coincidence or whether you believe that there is no such thing as a "coincidence." There's certainly no scientific evidence to support it. It's a myth of a perceived reality. My reality is that everything happens for a reason. That there are otherworldly realms beyond our understanding, beyond our perception of reality, which appear to work behind the scenes. Someone certainly gave me evidence of that. Looking back, I had to wonder—were they laying the groundwork for me, knowing one day I'd want to be a medium?

CHAPTER 6

There's a Religion for This?

My (not so) tall, (hardly) dark, and (all things being relative) handsome genealogy buddy Dwight, who is about my age, studies different religions as a pastime. We had traveled to Ireland twice together for our client, and during one of those trips, he introduced me to the religion of Spiritualism and mediumship. I served as the editor of the National Genealogical Society's *NewsMagazine* then, and he asked if he could write an article on researching Spiritualist ancestors.

I've always been somewhat of a risk-taker—some would say troublemaker—in my genealogy career, writing articles on less politically correct ancestral topics, such as the prevalence of abortion in the nineteenth century among middle- and upper-class married women. Now I imagined a magazine cover for a publication of that century-old staunch society featuring a Ouija board. Splendid article pitch, Dwight! From the emails I received after the article appeared, I discovered many genealogists had Spiritualist ancestors.

Dwight explained that Spiritualism's central tenet is the belief that consciousness survives physical death and that, through mediums, we can communicate with the spirits of the dead. Spiritualists don't "conjure the dead," he explained. It's a mutually agreeable communication.

He gave me the religion's historical background, and I learned more when he submitted the article. Spiritualism was a widespread religious movement in the nineteenth and early twentieth century. Of course, the belief in the spirits, and communicating with them, has been around for eons, regardless of specific faith; all religions believe in some form of afterlife. Even pre-Christian lore was filled with ghostly visitations, and any Christian can tell you that the human called Jesus of Nazareth arose from the dead and made postmortem visits to his apostles. Spiritualists point to numerous passages in both the Old and New Testaments that address and support spirit communication.

Back when Dwight wrote his article in 2004, Spiritualism didn't call to me as a religious practice, and I wasn't yet on the path of trying to become a medium. But the history and the correlation between the rise of Spiritualism and the start of the women's rights movement interested me.

The birth of modern Spiritualism stemmed from two teenage sisters, Margaret "Maggie" and Kate Fox, of Hydesville, New York, in March 1848. Word traveled fast that they had communicated with the dead through raps they heard on the walls of their parents' home. With the assistance of their mother, the senior Margaret Fox, they worked out an alphabet with the spirit so the raps could be translated into words. The spirit who visited the Fox sisters claimed to be that of a peddler, Charles B. Rosna, who had been murdered in the house. He wanted to let the family know he'd been buried in the cellar.

After one attempt to uncover the body failed due to rising water as they dug, the girls' father and another man took their shovels to the basement in July of that year and dug again. This time, they unearthed broken pottery, strands of hair, and bone fragments. Skeptics believed these were animal bones, and that no peddler named Charles B. Rosna existed. Fifty-six years later, in 1904, schoolchildren playing in the abandoned Fox "spook" house discovered a crumbling cellar wall. When it gave way, a human skeleton revealed itself. A doctor estimated that the bones were at least fifty years old. While not conclusive proof that the skeleton belonged to Rosna, this was an interesting "coincidence."

The Fox sisters found themselves in demand for their abilities, and they endured many tests from skeptics—from having their feet and hands bound while communicating with the dead to being examined in only their underclothing by trustworthy women before and after séances. They passed all tests.

Real trouble arose in 1888, though, when Maggie Fox confessed that it was all a hoax and that the rapping noises came from the sisters cracking their knuckles, which echoed in the silence of the séance parlor. She and her sister, Kate, later tried to recant the confession, but it hardly mattered. By then, spirit communication was widespread and popular. The religious movement she and her sister had inspired not only flourished but spread to England via the American medium Maria B. Hayden, then on to other countries. Now a new religion had been exported from America rather than imported. If anything, the sisters' confession, along with the rise in charlatan mediums, helped prompt Spiritualism to establish criteria to test and authenticate the validity of mediums.

During the same time that the Fox sisters unknowingly started a religious movement, the women's rights movement gained momentum in America. The first Women's Rights Convention was held in July 1848 in Seneca Falls, New York, just four months after the Fox sisters first heard raps on the walls of their house. The women's movement I already knew about. I researched it to write my book *A Genealogist's Guide to Discovering Your Female Ancestors*. But I didn't recall any mention of the tie with the Fox sisters and how this new religious movement of Spiritualism provided women with a voice, where they could assert their independence, as opposed to mainstream, male-dominated religions. Most mediums were, and still are, women. Talking to the dead offered them a new profession and provided single and widowed women with the opportunity for financial stability. Some mediums worked in front of audiences of thousands. This gave them a public platform to speak about women's issues, reform movements, abolition, and temperance, as well as provide messages from the dead. Others, like Maria B. Hayden, held private séances.

Estimates claim that some two to three million people in the mid-nineteenth century were Spiritualists or believed in spirit communication. Spiritualism drew believers from different faiths, especially Universalists and Unitarians and, for a time, from Mormonism. William S. Godbe's wife became a medium, and thus the Godbeite movement began among some Mormons. But Spiritualism for Mormons presented a problem. Parley P. Pratt in 1853 wrote, "If on the one hand we admit the principle of communication between the spirit world and our own, and yield ourselves to the unreserved or indiscriminate guidance of every spiritual manifestation, we are liable to be led about by every wind of doctrine, and by every kind of spirit which constitute the varieties of being and of thought in the spirit world."

Funny how Spiritualists didn't see this as a problem. They believed those in spirit communicated harmonious messages. The Mormon leaders, though, decided it was better to rely on the superiority and authority of only their human male priesthood to communicate with the unseen world.

Many famous people converted to Spiritualism or were "friends" of Spiritualism, including Elizabeth Barrett Browning, William Butler Yeats and his love, Maude Gonne, James Fenimore Cooper, Sir Arthur Conan Doyle (who wrote, along with his Sherlock Holmes series, a two-volume work titled *The History of Spiritualism*), Thomas Edison, Horace Greeley, Victor Hugo, Harriet Beecher Stowe, Daniel Webster, and Abraham and Mary Todd Lincoln. Today, people might be shocked to learn that our president hosted séances in the White House to seek counsel from the spirit world, but that did happen during Lincoln's administration.

The popularity of spirit communication by women, especially after major wars—the Civil War, World War I, and World War II—was understandable. It was they who lost husbands, sons, and brothers. The rise, too, in women seeking messages from the departed, either themselves as mediums or in engaging the services of a medium, came at a time when infant mortality was high. Illnesses, diseases, and accidents took the lives of many children. Death abounded during the Victorian era. It's no wonder women and men yearned to continue the bond with their beloved children and family members.

Spiritualism's growth in America suffered, however, for lack of a visionary or charismatic leader like the other two American-born religions: Mormonism, which had the prophet Joseph Smith, and Christian Science, which had Mary Baker Eddy (a former Spiritualist). Instead, Spiritualism spread through Spiritualist mediums, who became itinerant representatives of the religion, touring the country and giving readings to large crowds. These "message services" offered not only communication from deceased loved ones but also a lecture on Spiritualism. One of the most popular speakers was English-born Emma Hardinge Britten, who traveled the world spreading the Spiritualist message and authored several books. She became the pioneer most revered by the British Spiritualists, offering seven simple principles she'd received from the spirit world that would form their religious philosophy.

As more questionable and fraudulent mediums capitalized on the opportunity to make a buck, however, true believers established Spiritualist communities or "camps" to offer mediumship development classes, to ordain ministers, and to test and authenticate individual mediums. The first in America was the Lily Dale Spiritualist Assembly, which convened in Lily Dale, New York, in 1879. At least twenty of these camps are still going strong today in the United States.

Spiritualism attracted followers not only for its belief in the afterlife and the ability to communicate with those who had departed but also because of its view of salvation: everyone, no matter how sinful, could be redeemed; and the concept that heaven and hell weren't physical places but rather states of consciousness. Yet the slow growth in the number of Spiritualist churches across the United States was further evidence of the religion's lack of organization. Although by 1855 some two million people followed the religion, the 1860 United States federal census listed only seventeen churches; by 1906, there were 455 churches in America with membership in the tens of thousands. After World War II, Spiritualism greatly declined in the United States but continued to thrive in the United Kingdom.

I took another look at the website for the National Spiritualist Association of Churches here in America. Maybe I had missed something that would help me. This was the twenty-first century; surely they had virtual classes for those who didn't live by a church. Not seeing anything on the site, I emailed. When someone responded by saying they would have a "missionary" contact me, I recoiled as if scalded by boiling holy water. Since we lived in Utah surrounded by Mormons, the word missionary conjured visions of Book-of-Mormon-thumpin' young male missionaries in white dress shirts and black nametags announcing, "Elder So-and-So," sent into the world to knock on doors and convert the unsaved masses. Sorry, Spiritualists. Maybe you're not the right path for me.

CHAPTER 7

Genealogists Have Always Connected with the Dead

I was two months into my quest, yet I still hadn't found my tribe—a group or someone, anyone, who could help me become a medium. I wasn't sure I could do this on my own. I had Jim's support, but I still yearned for other like-minded people, mainly because I inadvertently distanced myself from everyone else. When I embarked on this journey, Dwight had warned me: "All I have to say is the more you get into this, the more you will find yourself distant from just about everyone around you. Are you prepared for that?"

I scoffed at his comment at the time, even saying that the people I'd told so far seemed fascinated that I was trying to talk to the dead. Little did I know that "fascinated" wasn't the right word; "miffed" and "amused" were more like it.

My tendency to thrust myself into a new passion—like a parched Israelite wandering in the desert for forty years who finally finds an oasis—reminded me of when I first became addicted to genealogy. The thrill and excitement of the ancestor hunt was so compelling that all I talked about was "ancestor this and ancestor that." That's when I realized that there were two types of people in this world: genealogists and non-genealogists. Not everyone was interested in the past and dead people. No wonder genealogists were a tight-knit group; like attracts like, and only those with the same passion for ancestor hunting could understand our drive and motivation. Non-genealogists couldn't comprehend that jubilant feeling when a death certificate arrived in the mail and the cause of death was unusual.

I remembered this same passion as more strange things happened to me. Much of what spewed forth from my mouth now was "Spirit this and Spirit that" and "Oh, another thing that happened . . ." Dear God! Had I become a born-again Spiritualist?

People had always trusted and believed what I'd told them. I'd been an authority in the field of genealogy during my long career, and as a writer and educator, I now taught graduate students creative nonfiction writing. Colleagues and students viewed me as an expert, as someone they'd seek for advice and wisdom, as someone they'd hire for a writing or editing project or refer clients to. Even when I selectively shared stories of my experiences, some kindly listened, but a few mocked me. Why weren't they taking me seriously? Was Dwight correct? Was I distancing myself from friends and family because I accepted the scientific and empirical evidence for consciousness survival, and they didn't?

Each time I shared my mediumship aspiration with someone, it felt as if I were "coming out." I never knew what reaction I'd get. Those who accepted the idea of an afterlife, either because of their beliefs or an experience they'd had, asked to hear more and usually shared their own stories. Skeptics asked no questions; they smiled and waited for the punch line. Born-again Christians—ah, yes, well, they were another story. No smiles there. One such individual quoted to me in emails scriptures that spirit communication was all the devil's doing, and that if, say, his father communicated, it would actually be the devil impersonating him. What? And would the devil be bringing messages of love and healing to lead him astray? That didn't sound like the devil's MO.

This person obviously hadn't read or remembered the passages in the Bible that discuss spirit communication and mediumship as a good thing.

According to *Spiritualism in the Bible* by E. W. and M. H. Wallis, "The word 'medium' in the sense in which it is used by Spiritualists had not been adopted when King James's translators did their work, or it would probably have been used in many important passages," so Spiritualists interpret "prophets" in the Bible as "mediums." A prophet is someone who, according to the dictionary, is "regarded as an inspired teacher or proclaimer of the will of God." Because Spiritualists believe that spirit communication is sanctioned by God, mediums are doing God's work, and the messages from deceased loved ones are born of "the word of God."

In one historical Spiritualist newspaper, trance medium Emma Frances Jay said in 1855,

How did Christ receive many of the instructions he gave? Were they not influxes from higher sources than himself, or utterances from Spirits that surrounded him? Are there not repeated evidences of his holding converse with Spirits? Did not Paul, John, and in fact, almost every one of the prophets and apostles, yea, and the patriarchs, receive their instructions from spiritual sources? What is called inspiration is no more nor less than a compliance with the laws and a realization of the results of spiritual converse, and it is through this that you have received every iota of knowledge in relation to the spiritual powers and a future life.

This person emailing me must have also forgotten that Jesus, an ordinary man with extraordinary abilities, came back from the dead just to prove an afterlife existed. Jesus allegedly said, "He who believes in me, the works that I do, he will do also; and greater works than these he will do." Wasn't that the whole premise behind the slogan "What would Jesus do?" The emails from this person were so wrought with negativity, it nearly caused my eyeballs to ignite in flames as I read them. I finally cut off the communication. A healthy, open-minded debate is one thing, but this went nowhere.

As a genealogist, I know of people who have had a personal or family history with, shall we say, "imitation" mediums. One, as a teenager, told fortunes based on people's reactions and body language. This was called a "cold reading," I'd later learn, a series of techniques that fake mediums, psychics, mentalists, and carnival fortune-tellers used to convince someone they know more than they do. They rely on high-probability guessing, observation, and picking up on unconscious signals from the person seated in front of them. Of course, shady people abound in many fields, from lawyers to investment brokers.

Another had a grandmother who often invited a medium to the house for séances. The medium would tie a scarf around her eyes so tight it caused the skin above and below to bulge. Mentalists back in the day used this blindfold technique to "read" questions in sealed envelopes. Johnny Carson created his Carnac the Magnificent routine based on this premise. One legitimate mentalist was Dr. Richard Ireland, and clips of his demonstrations from the *Rob Allen Show* are on YouTube. Allen was a skeptic until he attempted to trick Ireland but discovered the joke was on him. Allen became a believer in psychic phenomena after that.

But I soon learned there's a difference between a psychic and a medium. A psychic connects with a living person to "read" their aura—that is, the invisible energy field that is part of us all. Within that aura is everything we've experienced from our past and present, as well as our hopes and desires. A good psychic reads these in a person's aura, but they cannot predict the future. If a psychic tells you that you will meet the love of your life next Wednesday, but next Wednesday the love of your life comes down with the flu and doesn't leave home, that prediction ends up like a decomposing fly carcass on the windowsill. The other glitch is a psychic can also sense from the aura your desires, so she or he could make a prognostication based on that without realizing it. All a psychic can predict are probabilities of someone's future based on past and present decisions and actions.

A medium, on the other hand, is the mediator between this world and the next. Mediums connect with the souls of those in the spirit world. Back in the days of the Fox sisters, the phenomena came through as raps and other noises; today, mediums use mental mediumship. They communicate with a deceased loved one through not just mental telepathy but a soul-to-soul and heart-to heart telepathy. No, not a physical heart. A spiritual heart connection.

Not all psychics are mediums, but all mediums are psychics, which is why it's redundant for someone to call themselves a "psychic medium." Mediums use their psychic faculties to communicate with the spirit world, and as I discovered, it's those psychic abilities that often awaken first.

Although my mom was now in the spirit world, my father had retired to Florida. He was in his early eighties when I started my journey but looked like he was in his sixties. He still had jet-black hair, compliments of L'Oréal. Jim and I visited him about every other year. My dad would always start a conversation about his demise with "If, God forbid, I should die . . ." He was the kind of person to ensure that all his affairs were properly in order and his wishes carried out. He told me on more than one occasion not to hesitate to "pull the plug."

"What if you're not hooked up to anything?" I'd ask.

"Then hook me up and pull the plug!"

He had a far greater fear of languishing in a nursing home than dying. His belief had long been that "when you're dead, you're dead." I told him over the phone one day that evidence shows that our consciousness survives physical death, that we live on in spirit after our physical bodies die. He said, "Well, I believe what you're saying because you're my daughter. But if anyone else told me that, I'd think there was something wrong with them."

What was I supposed to do with a comment like that? Say, "Gee, thanks, Dad, I appreciate your unconditional support"? Mind you, this was a man who watched and *believed* everything he heard on Fox News, including that there was no scientific evidence for climate change.

Another skeptical friend said to me, "To convince me, you'd need a consensus within the scientific community and studies published in peer-reviewed journals." First, good luck on getting a consensus within the scientific community on much of anything. It took half a millennium for science to fully understand magnetism, they still don't have a consensus on what gravity is and how it works, and after decades and trillions of dollars, they also don't agree on the causes of most cancers or how to cure them. And second, there *are* studies, and meta-analyses of those studies, published in plenty of peer-reviewed journals. But as parapsychologist Loyd Auerbach said, "You can hand a skeptic all the scientific studies, and all they will see are blank pages."

I debated the science ad nauseam with friends and Laurie. "Yeah, well, my science can beat up your science" seemed to be the argument on both sides. As Einstein once said, "Science without religion is lame. Religion without science is blind." But their minds were made up based on "materialistic monism"—that is, everything is made of matter, and from matter everything else emerges, including energy, consciousness, personalities, and emotions.

In the words of quantum physics pioneer Wolfgang Pauli, "It is my personal opinion that in the science of the future, reality will neither be 'psychic' nor 'physical' but somehow both and somehow neither." Or as Deepak Chopra puts it, "The issue is not either/or, but both/and."

Why can't we all play nice and realize that the materialists and the paranormal scientists might both be right? The paranormal community is willing to accept this possibility, so why not the skeptics? Healthy skepticism is fine; a closed mind to any other possibilities frightens me.

I'd had one particularly draining morning of debates with Laurie—who emailed afterward, "I love you, always will, but we will *never* see eye to eye on this stuff. We'll just have to agree to disagree." Uh-oh. I'd pushed her too far. Not only would we have to agree to disagree, but I'd have to learn how to keep my mouth shut. I never dreamed there would be something we couldn't talk about. We hadn't had this much disparity in our relationship since Laurie called to announce that she and her husband had adopted—I can barely speak the words—a *dog*. She knew we had a family tradition of cats. While my mother and I didn't agree on much, we'd both been cat people.

"Why didn't you get a cat?" I asked Laurie.

"I'm allergic to cats."

"Since when? We've always had cats."

"I know. Didn't you notice my eyes were always red and watery?"

"I thought you'd been drinking."

"When I was *five*?"

I said to Jim, "I'm so tired of talking to skeptics. If like attracts like, where are all the like-minded souls? Why aren't I attracting them?"

My word was now being doubted, questioned, and derided. Did I live in the Dark Ages? Would I be torched at the stake? Locked away in an insane asylum? I grew more defensive, feeling as if my intelligence was open to distrust and ridicule. It's quite a shock to have people you've known for a long time suddenly, and for the first time, doubt your word and your sanity. Rather than jeopardize friendships and, more importantly, my confidence, I decided not to talk to anyone else about spirit communication or my journey to become a medium.

That lasted two hours and forty-nine seconds.

We went to dinner that evening with two out-of-town genealogy friends, Fran and Olivia, both Southern ladies in their sixties, visiting Salt Lake City to research at the Family History Library. I didn't know what they believed or didn't believe, but I wasn't about to have another conversation with myself about spirits while other people politely nodded and wondered when poor Jim would have me committed. As the evening wound down, I mentally patted myself on the back for not saying the word *spirit* the whole time.

The waiter brought our checks. Our table drew quiet while everyone pulled out their credit cards.

"What time is it?" I leaned over and asked Jim.

"Eight fifteen."

"Oh, good. We'll make it home in time for my TV show."

I thought I had said it softly enough that no one else heard me. We'd come to Red Lobster, and the place hummed with conversations and the clang of dinnerware around us. Our friends had sharp hearing.

"What show is that?" Olivia asked.

I hesitated, looked at Jim, then said, "*Ghost Adventures.*" I hoped to leave it at that, but our tired-looking friends perked up. They each had their own spirit stories to share. When I mentioned my latest toy, the SB-7 Spirit Box—an external voice box ghost hunters used to communicate with the other side, which I never could get to work—Fran wanted to know where to get one so she could take it to the cemetery. Olivia asked my advice about ridding herself of a negative energy that had attached itself to her. "Just be firm," I said, "and tell it to leave." What she said next nearly caused me to drop dead from apoplexy: "It's so refreshing to know someone intelligent who believes in ghosts!"

Was it in part because we were all genealogists who dealt with the dead on a daily basis that we had come to accept the existence of an afterlife? In many families, there seemed to be only one person afflicted and impassioned about discovering ancestors. Why that one person? Why weren't other family members usually as interested, or interested at all, in their heritage with the same degree of enthusiasm and obsession? When that one person opened the genealogy portal, did ancestral spirits take notice?

One of our colleagues and a dear friend, Henry Z Jones Jr., authored two books in the 1990s, one called *Psychic Roots: Serendipity and Intuition in Genealogy* and the other *More Psychic Roots: Further Adventures in Serendipity and Intuition in Genealogy* (or what his friends fondly called *Bride of Psychic Roots*). Hank had his own serendipitous and intuitive experiences in researching Palatine ancestors, those from the Palatinate region of Germany who had settled in Ireland at the encouragement of the English in 1709. He published *The Palatine Families of Ireland* while an undergraduate at Stanford University in 1965, but then, as he wrote in the introduction to *Psychic Roots*, he "felt compelled to move on and chronicle all of the 847 Palatine families who bypassed Ireland and arrived in colonial New York in 1710." To his knowledge, he was not related to anyone in this second group, and he knew nothing about their origins in Germany nor where to begin looking.

Hank hired German genealogist Carla Mittelstaedt-Kuraseck, whom he directed to go across villages in the Palatinate region to try and document the origins of these emigrants. Hank didn't care where she began, so he randomly chose a person named Dieterich Schneider and told Carla to start searching, oh, how about in the Westerwald region at Hachenburg? As he would later discover, Schneider was the only emigrant in the study to whom Hank was related.

The weirdness didn't stop there. Hank began to have dreams about dead Palatines. An emigrant would appear to him, telling Hank where the person had come from. At first, Hank didn't give the dreams any credence; then, for the heck of it, he'd have Carla pursue what the emigrant had told him. In several cases, that's where Carla found the emigrant's origins. As Hank says, "I don't chase dead Germans; they chase me!" After the publication of the first volume of *Psychic Roots*, his story aired on *Unsolved Mysteries*.

Psychic Roots came about because Hank wondered if other genealogists had similar experiences. He put out a call to three hundred "of the world's leading family historians" to share their stories. In the first volume, he published true tales from 120 contributors. He concluded that volume by inviting readers to share their experiences for a second volume. In *More Psychic Roots*, he published three hundred additional contributions. Hank's books came out in the 1990s, before the internet boom, when the genealogical community was still relatively small.

The responses Hank received didn't come just from maiden aunts—what we call the grassroots genealogists—whom living family members already thought were a little off. They also came from reputable and well-respected researchers in the field of genealogy, many with advanced degrees and science backgrounds, some of whom I never suspected would believe in such things as serendipity, intuition, and ancestral ghosts. I didn't need to worry about "coming out" to other genealogists. Sure, there would be some skeptics, but Hank had opened the door for me and those of us who believed there was a reason our ancestors had chosen us to be the family history caretakers.

As you might expect, many genealogists' paranormal experiences took place in cemeteries, but equally as many took place in various research repositories. Genealogists in Hank's books tell of randomly pulling a book from a shelf and it falling open to a page on which their ancestor was listed. Or they'd accidently thread the wrong roll of microfilmed records onto a reader, only to discover their ancestor among those documents. Or, like Hank, ancestors appeared to them in dreams, telling them where to look for records.

I contributed two stories to *More Psychic Roots*, one of which I wrote about in my essay, "Waking the Dead," and published in my memoir, *Inheriting the Gordon Hips*. It's about my serendipitous meeting with a genealogist in a rural New York cemetery when I was about ten. I can promise you that I never once thought, either before or for years after that meeting, that I wanted to be a professional genealogist when I grew up. A writer, definitely. A mortician, sure. A lion tamer, maybe. A genealogist, no. Yet a career in genealogy led me on a path where I achieved those first two childhood goals: I became a writer, and I worked with the dead.

The second story I sent Hank also involved a cemetery. Laurie's dad and I visited Dade County, Missouri, one July, searching cemeteries for his ancestors. I knew one of his ancestors was buried in a particular cemetery because I had found a book of headstone transcriptions that gave her gravestone inscription. We walked row after row, reading stones, but couldn't find her marker. We took a break under the only tree planted there. My husband sat on one of the headstones while I stood, sipping a bottle of water and feeling exasperated that I couldn't find this one marker. About to begin our hunt again, I looked down and saw that my husband sat on a marker right next to his ancestor, the one we had been seeking all morning.

It dawned on me as I embarked on this journey that genealogists have always had a unique communication with their dead relatives. Some genealogists were just more open to the idea and aware of the subtle or not-so-subtle signs of them talking to us. I wondered if I could make that connection even stronger by becoming a medium.

CHAPTER 8

Team Sharon

When Jim and I started dating, I wasn't religious, yet I found an odd comfort knowing we both had a Catholic upbringing. He was also a nonpracticing Catholic, but had been an altar boy in his early years, and his maternal uncle had been a priest. With Jim, I felt a need I'd never experienced before: I yearned for a spiritual connection with him. We tried going to Mass together a few times, but Catholicism no longer fit either of us. The last Mass we attended, at the cathedral in Salt Lake City, was on a St. Patrick's Day, which happened to fall on a Sunday. Being Irishophiles, we wore green and anticipated a sermon on how St. Patrick drove the snakes out of Ireland and brought the faith in. Mexican-born Father Hernandez, however, didn't mention a single python, or even utter the name of the patron saint of Ireland. This was the final pluck on our Gaelic harp strings, and we left disenchanted.

We hadn't discussed religion or spirituality much in the time we'd been together, so it surprised me that Jim was open to the whole spirit communication idea and willing to meditate with me when I decided to become a medium. Like most Catholics, he believed in an afterlife and that our loved ones remained with us. Catholics, although they don't necessarily think of it this way, are brought up with a reverence for spirits.

Talking and praying to the saints is fine. But talking with Grandma in the spirit world and getting advice from her, well, not so much.

Jim's Catholic upbringing made him open to supporting me on my journey and participating with me in some of it. He had no desire to become a medium himself, but he didn't consider me loony for wanting to give it a go.

For our ten-minute daily meditation sessions, we'd need a timer that didn't tick and, of course, candles. It seemed we wouldn't meditate properly without candles burning, even though our eyes were closed and we couldn't see the candles. But we could smell them. Jim and I had spent what felt like a significant part of our lives in Walmart, sniffing for the perfect meditation candles. But what scent would most likely attract the spirits? Plain vanilla? Cinnamon bun? Apple pie? Pumpkin pie? Cranberry, mashed potatoes, and roast turkey? We left with unscented candles.

Our TV and sitting room became the TV and sitting and meditating room. To make it official, I hung a framed poster of Salvador Dali's *Meditative Rose* over the television, between the two bookcases. We sat upright in our blue recliners. The idea was not to get so comfortable that you'd fall asleep, but you also didn't want your extremities twisted pretzel-style as in traditional yoga meditation poses. For spirit communication, the energy from and into your body must flow easily. I lit two candles, set the timer for ten minutes, then we sat with eyes closed and palms upward on our thighs to allow spirit energy to enter.

Meditation virgins that Jim and I were, we performed the first suggested exercise in one of my spirit-communication books, which was supposed to fill the ten-minute session. We took several deep breaths, then slowed our breathing. We worked from toes to head, relaxing each body part. Then I peeked at the timer. It had been only a minute. I always was a quick study. I mentally moved on to another meditation exercise I remembered from my reading, leaving Jim with the first one. In this one, you're supposed to connect with nature (always nature) and visualize a happy place where you will meet your spirit guides. I imagined walking the tree-lined drive to my great-grandmother's house in Ireland. When I approached the front door, for some reason I couldn't get myself inside the house. I suspected it was likely because I had no memory associated with it, as I'd never been inside. No spirit guided me in. I invited my spirit guides to meet me outside. I lingered in the garden by the daffodils and waited. All was still and quiet. Peaceful. *Meditation might actually be enjoyable*, I thought.

Then Jim snorted. His head was rolled against the recliner back, mouth agape. No wonder the spirits hadn't come. He scared them away with his snoring.

According to my mediumship books, we each have a gaggle of spirit guides, and these are the spirits you should try to contact first and ask for their help. (I'm not sure what the correct collective term is for a group of spirit guides, but gaggle seems as good as any.) American Spiritualists say that we each have, at a minimum, five personal guides. These are known as the inner band guides: a joy guide, who ensures our happiness; a protector guide, who protects us from negative spirit energies and keeps us safe; a chemist guide, who helps with our physical and mental wellbeing; a doctor-teacher guide, who guides our learning; and a master guide, who helps us along the path to enlightenment.

We might have other specialized personal guides, depending on our callings and talents, such as a muse guide for artists and writers. Another guide is the gatekeeper, who typically does double duty as one of the five inner guides. The gatekeeper admits or denies other spirits' access to you as a medium. I preferred to call this guide my bouncer. While our family, friends, and other loved ones who've crossed over might make contact, watch over us, and run interference at times, they're usually not one of these guides. Beyond that, there are higher levels of ascended master guides, angels, and outer band guides.

This was quite the corporate structure; I realized I'd need a flow chart to keep them straight. But this number of otherworldly guides didn't surprise me. I'm pretty high maintenance anyway. Team Sharon, I called them. It became clear to me, though, that my math guide realized that he never stood a chance and resigned as soon as he could. In fact, I suspect none of my spirit guides had any clue what they were getting themselves into when they saw my wee, fat, pathetic soul standing on the grade school playground, the last to be chosen for any teams. "Oh, all right," they said, "we'll take Sharon."

Even mediums who aren't Spiritualists by faith say they have spirit guides, so this wasn't a belief based on a lone prophet's word or a particular religion but on the messages mediums have received from the spirit world. These spirit guides have volunteered to work with each of us as part of their own soul's growth and journey, a sort of community-service position, or maybe it's for penance. Who knows? Through the law of attraction—that is, like attracts like—our spirit guides share like energy with us, just as we are attracted to and share interests with our friends here in the physical world. Our guides typically lived in the physical world at some point, so they're able to guide us based on their own firsthand experience, as well as through their wisdom from the great beyond.

Some higher-level entities, such as angels, have never existed in human form but are divinely created by God. Angels vibrate at a super high rate, even higher than a hummingbird, so they aren't visible either to the physical eye or the psychic eye. Interestingly, mediums in trance often bring communication from spirit guides, but not from angels. That's because angels do not do the work of spirit guides. They have a higher calling. What we call a "guardian angel" is more likely a "spirit guardian." These spirit guardians remain with us through life.

Generally, our spirit guides will not interfere with our lives unless asked. They recognize that we have free will. They guide, not push.

They might come through in what we'd call a hunch, a gut feeling, or intuition. Whether we follow that nudge is up to us. Many people, even nonbelievers, have reported feeling as if someone looked out for them during a crisis situation.

When Laurie's dad and I moved to Colorado Springs after living in Florida for the previous six years, I had no doubt someone had been watching over me. A delivery man had come to the door and left a package at the bottom of the steps that led up to house. The porch was icy, and I wasn't accustomed to walking on ice. With my first step, my feet flew out in front of me, and my back slammed onto the edge of the concrete step. I couldn't move and thought I'd surely broken my spine.

The intense pain subsided within a minute. I stood up, had no problem moving, and climbed back up the steps, holding the package and the wrought-iron railing. I expected to be sore and bruised the next day. I wasn't. Given the impact, I can't explain why I hadn't broken my back or had any side effects. I suspect now, though, that when I slipped, the guide in charge must've dozed off, snoring away in his otherworldly recliner, and corrected the mistake by healing me instantly.

Even as I write now about all these spirit guides, it still sounds kind of goofy to me. It feels as if I'd just written, "I believe in leprechauns, the tooth fairy, Santa Claus, the Easter Bunny, Bigfoot, and little green aliens. So there." I consider myself a reasonably intelligent person, not easily gullible. I don't believe everything I read or see on TV, like those infomercials for cellulite creams that make your thighs look taut and smooth. (Okay, long ago I did fall for one of those.) If something doesn't make logical sense to me, I am skeptical until I acquire more information. I don't believe ludicrous statements, such as a woman's body can repel a rapist's sperm, so therefore she can't get pregnant. I don't fly in the face of scientific evidence and insist, like some people, that evolution doesn't exist and climate change is just liberal fear tactics. I am a critical thinker who does my best not to see the world in black and white or right and wrong. I also have a medical, and therefore scientific, background. Yet, as weird as all these individual personal spirit guides sounded, I had no trouble accepting their existence and that they're here for me. And why not? They're every egotist's dream team.

Having this gaggle of personal spirit guides makes more sense to me than the mainstream Judeo-Christian belief that there is one personal supernatural being, a.k.a. God, who's the only employee at the cable company's customer service phone center during an internet outage and is fielding millions of lines ringing simultaneously. My spirit guides have one main job in the afterlife, and that's to guide and look after me. And if not a village, it takes at least a team.

The books on mediumship development include meditations to meet your spirit guides. You envision walking along a beach or nature path (boy, these meditations were repetitive and unimaginative), then eventually you'd see someone coming toward you who would be one of your guides. A bench would magically appear so you could sit and have this blissful conversation with your guide, during which they'd tell you their name and give you a divine message. It sounded great but never worked for me or Jim.

Being of little patience, I finally asked my spirit bouncer for his or her name. I heard "Violet." Not exactly the name I expected for a big burly guy in black. What kind of bouncer muscle would a spirit named Violet have to keep out negative entities? *Well, duh*, I thought. *I bet that's a nickname. The full name is probably Vito "The Violet" Castellano.* The books say guides really don't care what you call them. Since Jim didn't have any luck with a name, he decided he'd call his gatekeeper "Carlton," after the unseen doorman on the 1970s TV show *Rhoda*.

After learning more about guides and the afterlife, though, I concluded that it couldn't have been my mom who made the van's transmission grind so we wouldn't break down in Wyoming on the way home from her memorial service. For one, Mom was only four days dead at that point. She might not have even realized yet that she was dead. Mom probably still hung out for a while in her room at the nursing home, watching *Judge Judy*, asking if it was lunchtime yet, and yelling at the nurses' aides that she had to pee. For another, Mom had no automotive skills. Just because you leave your body behind and become a spirit, it doesn't mean you magically know how to do things you didn't know how to do in the physical world. Now, if it had been a squeaky sewing machine belt, Mom knew how to fix that.

More than likely, our travel savior had been one of our protector guides or spirit guardians. Probably a guide had sent me signs of my mother's spiritual milestones through the lily blossom, knowing I observed it.

When we die, we retain our personalities. This is how you know whether you're receiving a message from a loved one or not. The message has to be in harmony with their character traits from the physical world. That's what convinced me that my mom had instigated the change purse arriving for my birthday, five months after her crossing. When it came to claiming money—even a dollar winnings from a lottery scratch card—all currency had an invisible magnetic field that pulled my mother to it. I was certain she had nudged the nursing home director that her change purse remained in the filing cabinet. That thirteen dollars was, after all, my rightful inheritance.

Once I learned about my guides, I called on them frequently. I asked them to help me keep my patience with my English Comp students when they wrote things like "I have a 10 year old son and a new edition on the way," or "I appalled you on your willingness to be an advocate," or "Art is in the eye of the be hollered." I now understood the saying "Patience is a virtue."

CHAPTER 9

Weird Stuff Keeps Happening

While visiting Laurie in Oregon seven months into my quest, I worked one afternoon in our motel room. As I sat on the olive-drab, woven-woolen couch, I was overcome with menstrual cramps and had to lie down. I had that crampy feeling not only in my lower abdomen but also in my back and an achiness in my upper thighs. There was only one problem: I hadn't had a period in more than three years. I kept thinking, *Why do I have menstrual cramps?* The answer popped into my head: *These are Laurie's cramps.* No sooner had the thought arrived than the cramps left.

We visited for my granddaughter's first birthday, and that evening, we all met for an early dinner at an Asian restaurant: me, Jim, Laurie, her husband, her baby daughter, my ex-husband, and his wife. It was a casual restaurant. Laurie had on jeans and a cute top. She'd always worn minimal jewelry—a petite necklace, her claddagh ring I had bought for her on one of my trips to Ireland, and her Hawaiian wedding band. I, on the other hand, probably looked like I was morphing into a gypsy fortune-teller with strands of crystals around my neck and beaded crystal bracelets.

The dining area was empty, and the hostess sat us at a round table, so conversation was easy for all to hear. During a lull, when the only sounds were glasses being raised to lips, I remembered the cramps from the afternoon. I found myself blurting out to Laurie seated next to me, "Are you on your period?"

Everyone sat with gaped mouths and poised hands, drinks held in midair. Laurie has always thought her mom a little wacky—she often calls me "freak"—and has never been surprised by what I might say. And, fortunately, she doesn't embarrass easily. Remember, she's a high school biology and anatomy teacher, and teaches the reproductive system to hormonal teenagers. On the first day of that lesson, she stands in front of her class and says, "Okay. Let's get the giggles out. Repeat after me: 'Penis, penis, penis. Vagina, vagina, vagina. Testicles, testicles, testicles.'" Despite this, Laurie looked a little startled when I asked if she was on her period. She let out a nervous laugh, and said, "Ah, yeah."

"When did your period start?" I transported to my old medical assisting days, interviewing a new patient.

Laurie rolled her eyes. "Yesterday."

"Okay then. I had your cramps this afternoon." I explained to her (and everyone else at the table) what I had experienced. "Don't you normally get cramps with your period?"

"Yeah."

"Did you get them this time?"

"No."

"There you have it then. Mystery solved," I said, quite pleased with myself.

Laurie, ever the scientist, searched for a logical explanation for me having cramps. She concluded that our hormones must have cycled together as girls who live together often do.

"Oh really?" I said. "I'm in menopause, remember? My hormones are made in a pharmacy, and my ovaries have shriveled to the size of raisins. I highly doubt it."

A month later, when her period arrived, she called to say she had cramps. "Can you take them for me again?"

"Sorry," I said. "It doesn't work for skeptics. Maybe if you had believed me last month . . ."

My resolve not to talk with Laurie about my journey didn't last long. She still thought everything I experienced was coincidence, or worse, that she'd need to find an institution for her mother soon. But Jim and I knew we must have opened some kind of portal to the other side.

"Did you move that book?" I asked Jim one afternoon at home.

We stood in our bedroom where we have four bookcases lining one wall. They each contain five shelves full of books, but this particular bookcase is visible from the bathroom. I'd noticed that the book, normally shelved on the bottom row with other general history books, had been placed two shelves up with women's history titles, and it lay on top of the others.

I have a photographic memory for where things are placed; I really should have been a continuity girl for movies or television. It's a skill I developed during my teen years. When I used to babysit, I'd grow bored late at night with kids asleep and nothing on TV, so I'd stand in different rooms and memorize where the parents kept things. The next time I went to babysit in that house, I'd test myself to see what had been moved. The out-of-place book on our bookcase also drew my attention because the book had a bright turquoise cover and spine. There was a vacant slot where the book had been on the lower shelf.

Jim picked up the book, *The Writer's Guide to Everyday Life in Colonial America*, and said he hadn't moved it. Neither of us currently researched any colonial ancestors, nor were we writing about them. It didn't make sense that Jim would have moved it. I knew I hadn't. That left only Figaro, and the feline wasn't talking.

So, like any other sane, rational, intelligent individual, I, of course, concluded that a colonial-era poltergeist showed interest in it. Perhaps he wanted to take a stroll down memory lane by reading a book about life in his day? I reshelved the book in its slot, then said aloud—while thinking to myself, *This is crazy*—"Whoever you are, it's okay to move this book again and to place it on this shelf." I patted the shelf where the book had recently sat. I wanted to acknowledge the spirit's presence so he'd know he'd gotten my attention. My mediumship books said that once spirits find a receptive person, it's possible to get vagabond souls passing through.

To ensure we had only nice spirits dropping by, the next day we bought from a metaphysical shop a bundle of white sage, a turkey tail feather, and an abalone shell to smudge the house and clear it of any negative energy. Smudging is a centuries-old American Indian custom. Jim had learned about smudging when he did genealogical and archival work for the Shakopee Mdewakenton Dakota Community in Minnesota. After leaving the tribe's archives, someone from the community would do this spiritual cleansing to remove any negativity.

I followed the directions tied to the bag, tore off a piece of the sage bundle, and placed it inside the shell. I lit the sage with a match. Thick, gray smoke arose from the shell; Jim and I coughed and gagged. I wasn't sure whether it's the smell or the smoke that does the trick. Both certainly made us want to leave.

Using the turkey feather, I fanned wisps of smoke away from us and around the house. As we cleansed the downstairs, I said in each room, "All negative energy must leave. Only positive energy is allowed to remain." Here was another quandary. Where does said "negative" energy go? To my neighbors' house? What if they're smudging, too, and their negative energy was coming into my house?

Going up the stairs, I fanned the smoke a little too fast; an ember blew out of the shell onto one of the carpeted steps. I could see the headlines: "Couple Ignites Condo while Exorcising Evil Spirits." I stomped out the ember right before the inferno engulfed us. Great. Now I had a black mark on the step and would see it each time I went up or down. When the white sage burned itself out, said the directions, this was the "all clear" indicator.

"It really stinks in here," Jim said, coughing and sneezing. Apparently, he's allergic to sage smoke. So much for smudging, which was just as well. The mechanics of it stymied me.

I told my bouncer in meditation that evening, "Okay. Here are the ground rules . . . In fact, you might want to start a notebook for these . . ." I'd read that you have to be specific with your guides, telling him or her what's acceptable and what's not. "No one evil comes around us." People are people, whether on this side or the other.

In reviewing my books, I discovered I'd been skipping a rather important step in our meditation ritual: When I called the meeting of Team Sharon to order, the first agenda item should be to ask spirit to encircle us with a protective layer of white light. Doing this allowed only positive energy to enter and would repel all negative energy, sort of the spirit world's version of spraying Yard Guard before spending time on the patio.

Another discovery I made was that each of us has control over spirits; no spirit controls us unless we let them. Negative energies feed off fear and will torment the person even more. If I sensed a negative energy around me, I needed to be firm and say, "You're not welcome here. You must leave." I could think of a few negative people I wanted to say that to as well.

I found the history Dwight had shared about Spiritualism interesting, but I was still leery about it as a religion and feared being hoodwinked. Yet I couldn't ignore that Spiritualist books by Spiritualist writers, both here in America and in England, kept falling in my path when I'd look for guidance on becoming a medium. The thought of a missionary contacting me, coming to my house and sitting in my living room, then telling me how I'd be saved if I became a Spiritualist, raised my dander. Yet I couldn't ignore the nudges pointing me in the direction of Spiritualism. So, what were they all about?

Searching online, I discovered Spiritualists believe in something greater than us mere mortals and all other spirit energies. American Spiritualists call it Infinite Intelligence; British Spiritualists call it Father God. God isn't the Sunday School God, though, perched on a throne, with the flowing white beard and doves flitting about him like Snow White. Whatever people label this supernatural being, Spiritualists believe it is a formless, shapeless, genderless, impersonal, omnipresent, omnipotent energy. They say it consists of pure unconditional love. They believe we are spirits created in that image of God, not a human-form image.

Much as I liked and agreed with Spiritualism's philosophy of a supernatural power of love, I had a problem with the word *God*. The term sounded so, well, religious. I also never liked New Age prayers that began "Father, Mother, God." I never had a tidy label for my beliefs. When I learned about pantheism not long before I had the idea to become a medium, it resonated with me more than the Christian God. There had to be a Master Mind of This Whole Mess. I chose to call it the Universe. When I learned that pantheists believe that the Universe is divine, nature is sacred, and everything is connected, that the overall energy we send out into the Universe, positive or negative, is what we receive back, it worked for me. Especially since I didn't have to get up on a Sunday morning and gather at the river. I felt content being spiritual, not religious, and as a pantheist, I eagerly awaited the time I'd be admitted to a hospital and see "pantheist" printed as my religion on my hospital bracelet.

The Universe also sounded genderless, more secular, more spiritual, even more scientific. The Universe wasn't angry and punitive, like the man-made God of my Catholic catechism days, who scared and guilted people into believing in Him (with a capital *H*) or you were damned to spend eternity in hell. The one who made Adam and Eve ashamed of their bodies and cast them from the Garden of Eden. The one who punished all women for Eve's sin by multiplying her pain in childbirth. (Gee, thanks, Eve.) The one who asked Abraham to kill his own son.

The one who made bad things happen to good people. The one who was jealous. The one who judged you and made you do penance before you'd be admitted into heaven. The one whose love was conditional. The one who allowed his only son (say, aren't we all children of God? I guess God has his favorites, too) to be sacrificed so human sins could be forgiven. How could a *loving* God do all these mean-spirited things? That's not love to me.

For Spiritualists—as with Buddhists, Taoists, and several other Eastern religions—there is no God who chooses on a whim whether to answer prayers or not and from whom you need to pass Go to collect heaven. "Our allegiance is not to a Creed, not to a Book, not to a Church, but to the Great Spirit of Life and to His eternal natural laws," said Silver Birch, a spirit guide who communicated in the 1930s through British trance medium Maurice Barbanell (1902–1981). Barbanell was the founder and editor of London's *Psychic News*. Through him, Silver Birch conveyed so much wisdom, recorded by someone who knew shorthand, that it resulted in a series of eighteen paperback books. I found and gradually purchased many of them, and they were surprisingly enjoyable to read. These books were the closest Spiritualists came to having a sanctified text, dictated directly from the spirit world.

Spiritualists believe in the laws of nature, such as the law of love, the law of attraction, the law of balance, and the law of cause and effect. A loving supreme being would *never* bring anyone pain or unhappiness. *We* make our own heaven or hell based on our choices and actions, either consciously or unconsciously. We have personal responsibility. Consequences come from our own doing. But what about those people who get cancer or dementia or are the victims of horrible crimes? These people hadn't done anything to deserve these awful consequences. Spiritualists say that before birth, when our soul chooses to inhabit a physical body, it will also choose a "life plan" intended to advance our spiritual growth and the growth of those around us. Souls who have chosen a life with dementia, for example, might be actually helping with life lessons for those around them here in the physical world. What's important is what we learn from the unfortunate experiences—as well as the pleasant ones—so we continue to grow spiritually.

According to Spiritualists, when our souls shed the physical body, there is no divine judgment; no one died for us to gain admittance into the next realm. Our souls, which are continuous, have the opportunity to reflect, grow, and learn from past mistakes—or not—just as we do during our physical lifetimes. Our souls, whether in physical or spirit form, have free will to eternally evolve and progress.

Heaven and hell aren't places but rather states of consciousness. The more our souls learn and grow in life and the afterlife, the higher the plane of consciousness we can achieve. The highest plane is, of course, being reincarnated as a cat. (I made that last part up—but think about it. Given the choice of playing the harp and singing hymns for eternity or being loved unconditionally and spoiled rotten like a cat for the next nine lives, which would you choose?)

While Christians believe that Jesus died so their sins could be forgiven, Spiritualists believe that there is no one to forgive you. Yes, there is compensation and retribution for your earthly deeds (what some call Karma), but you have a personal responsibility for all of your actions. If you want to achieve a higher plane after you die, to be closer to God, the Divine Spirit, or whatever you want to call it, then you have to accept responsibility for harm you've caused yourself and others and change your ways. This is why Spiritualists believe you would never want to commit suicide. Not only would you cross over with all the same problems you had on the earthly plane, but you'd have to atone to those you hurt in the physical world with your passing and to those who would have been touched by your life had you not taken it.

Some Spiritualists are Christian, but many aren't. They don't believe in Jesus Christ as a savior but do, however, acknowledge his human existence and have respect for his life and teachings. They believe that Jesus was the ultimate medium and healer. (I must confess: the skeptic in me questioned whether a man named Jesus walked the earth. In Kersey Graves's *The World's Sixteen Crucified Saviors*, he makes a compelling argument that Jesus wasn't an actual person but a myth created on earlier stories of deities or crucified saviors. Many of these pre-Christian saviors had strikingly similar life stories to Jesus: sons of a supreme god, virgin births, a December 25 birth date, stars pointing to their birthplace, shepherds and magi visiting, spending time in a desert. They, too, had disciples, performed miracles, were persecuted, resurrected, and appeared as apparitions. Will the real Jesus please stand up?)

As I learned more about Spiritualism, it sounded like a reasonable, commonsense religion. Of course, the part that intrigued me the most was that Spiritualists believe that when we leave the physical world, we take with us our thoughts, our personalities, our emotions, our intelligence, and our memories. We leave behind the casing, the physical body, that we had chosen to occupy for a given number of years based on our soul's personal and unique ongoing journey. We aren't bodies with souls, but souls with bodies. Just as we mourn our loss when a loved one passes, spirits, according to Spiritualist beliefs, mourn the departure of a spirit when a baby is born. These spirits know that they will be with that spirit again after the soul leaves the physical world, just as many of us know we will see our loved ones again when we cross back over to the spirit world. And they believe that those who've crossed over want to communicate with us, give us reassurance that they are still with us, and guide us; thus, they believe in a communion of spirits.

The religion adopted the sunflower as its symbol: "As the sunflower turns its face toward the light of the sun, so Spiritualism turns the face of humanity toward the light of truth."

Now to find all these lovely Spiritualist souls here on earth.

CHAPTER 10

Physical Phenomena

Members of my mother's family did not have long life spans. Her father died at age fifty-two and her mother at fifty-nine. Her siblings, aunts, and uncles mostly died in their fifties and early sixties. Had she not quit smoking in her sixties, the doctors told her, my mother wouldn't have lived as long as she did. While I had always hoped she'd make it to at least eighty, she was seventy-eight when she died. So, now on my path to communicate with the dead, the occasion of her eightieth birthday seemed like the perfect time to get this whole shebang going.

I lit the candles, then Jim and I assumed our meditation seats in our recliners and placed our palms upward on our thighs. I silently greeted spirit and called the meeting of Team Sharon to order, asking them to surround us in white light and that only positive energy be allowed to enter.

"Mom?" I asked mentally. "Are you here? I want to wish you a happy birthday."

I paused but received no mental response. I continued to talk to her in my mind. "Ma, can you blow out one of the candles for me?" I concentrated on the candles with everything I had, my eyes closed as I repeated over and over, "Ma, blow out the candle." My vibration level soared. I cheated and took a peek, the candle flame blurry but still glowing. "Ma," I implored, "blow out the candle." If there were a way for me to will it out, it would have happened. But nothing did. I asked my guides if my mom could give me some other sign, but again, nothing.

Disappointed, I went downstairs after our meditation time ended to make dinner, while Jim blew out the birthday candles and stayed upstairs. Spirits were busy entities, I reminded myself, and my mother always was stubborn and rarely listened to me.

I placed a sauté pan with some olive oil on the stove to heat. Then I added chopped onion and a few cloves of minced garlic. Jim said he can always tell he's in the right condo because his eyes water the minute he enters the door. That's the holy trinity to me: olive oil, garlic, and onions. They sizzled as I moved them around with a wooden spoon. A noise behind me drew my attention. Something brushed against the back of my right calf. I looked down, expecting to see the cat.

"Oh!" I stared at the basket of artificial geraniums that had been on top of the cabinet a few feet away. I looked up where the basket had been and said, "Hello!"

At the foot of the stairs, I called to Jim, "Come see what happened!"

As soon as he saw the flowers on the ground, he, too, knew what had happened.

I smiled. "Mom's here."

When our condo was under construction five years prior, after I picked out black kitchen appliances, a faux marble countertop, and dark wood cabinets, I decided to splurge on crown molding to give the cabinets a more finished look. There would be a two-foot clearance between the top of the cabinet and the ceiling, so before falling asleep each night, I would think about what to put up there. My dish pattern is Blue Willow china, and I had found dish towels imprinted with blue-and-white pottery, which included a bowl of bright-red apples and a water pitcher with greenery. That would be my color scheme, I decided.

The cabinetry is L-shaped, so when we moved in, I placed two large blue-and-white vases with artificial greenery at the ends, I put my antique Blue Willow platter I'd purchased in Ireland on a stand in the corner, and in between the platter and the vases, I placed two rectangular baskets that I had arranged with red silk geraniums. I dusted them once a month with a feather duster, and up until the occasion of my mother's eightieth birthday, they had remained sensibly secure in their proper place.

A few days prior to the basket-falling incident, I remembered looking at both baskets to make sure they weren't tilting after I had dusted them nearly two weeks prior. This was not my normal habit. Typically, I thought about them or noticed them only when dusting. I have no idea why I had the urge to consciously check them, since, as I've said, they've never fallen before. Both looked well and happy.

One air vent in the ceiling was seventeen inches from the other, non-falling basket. But the forced air coming from that vent in summer or winter has never caused that one to topple. The air from that vent certainly wouldn't have had the force to blow over the one that fell, which was eight feet away. Even if it had, the direction of the airflow would have blown it backward against the wall, not forward onto the floor. The basket was seated on the cabinet top, two and a half inches lower than the crown molding. To fall forward, it would require enough force from behind the basket to push it over the crown molding.

The incident occurred during winter, on January 21, so there were no open windows. The closest window to the falling basket was 20.4 feet away; a draft, even if we had one, could hardly be responsible.

Naturally, I told Laurie what happened. To prove to me there was a rational explanation and to confirm that her mother suffered from some kind of psychosis, she searched online for any seismic activity in our area around that time. We live along the Wasatch Fault, so that would be a logical possibility, but nothing else in the condo rattled or was disturbed. Much to her disappointment (I'm sure), there were no disturbances. As far as I know, there was no subterranean water that would cause earth movement, either. There were, of course, underground sewers, but again, nothing else moved that night. The two-story condo rested on a concrete slab foundation; we didn't have a basement.

We lived in a three-unit condo and had two wall neighbors, so perhaps one of my neighbors caused enough of a racket to disturb the flower basket. There were two problems with this hypothesis. First, we heard no noises coming from either neighbor, and if there had been enough commotion to cause something to move in our condo, surely we would have heard or felt it. Second, the wall behind the falling flower basket is not a neighboring wall. It's an interior wall.

The floor above the flower basket was the upstairs landing. Maybe the floor there vibrated when I walked on it, which caused the basket to take a nosedive. It's never done that before, but . . . Jim weighed more than I, so to debunk this idea, he went upstairs, directly above the basket, and jumped repeatedly. He then stomped up and down the stairs and even lunged against the wall opposite the kitchen cabinets and refrigerator. Thankfully, he didn't hurt himself pretending to be the police breaking down a door in a raid. None of this activity caused the basket to even tremble, so my petite steps on the landing or stairs wouldn't have triggered a delayed plunge.

Figaro, our retired, sixteen-year-old feline, no longer jumped higher than the bed. But he was also not in the kitchen when the basket came down. He had just had his dinner and busily groomed himself on a dining room chair.

The washing machine, dryer, and dishwasher were not operating at the time. The only electrical appliance turned on was the stove top.

There was no construction or road repair going on in our neighborhood then.

Perhaps vibrations from a passing truck caused it to fall. (I was intent on ruling out anything physical.) From my kitchen to the front street, it was fifty-five feet, and my kitchen was buffered by the condo entryway, laundry and bathroom area, the garage, and the driveway. We lived on a residential street in a small subdivision, so vehicles weren't traveling at more than twenty miles per hour. The main thoroughfare was 270 feet from us, but again, in five years, I've never had an incident of any trucks causing something in my house to vibrate or move. Because our condo was new and had such good insulation and tight windows, when the windows were closed, I couldn't hear traffic noise. Behind our condo was a Latter-day Saint church parking lot. While those Mormons can be a rowdy bunch on Sundays, it was empty that Monday evening.

We and our neighbors had electric garage doors, and when I sit upstairs in our meditation and TV room, I could faintly hear our door or the immediate neighbor's door open and close. I'd never noticed that this caused any vibration or movement in the condo, however, and our electric garage door motor was twenty-five feet from that kitchen wall.

Or maybe the vibrations came from a freight train. We lived 1.3 miles from railroad tracks. While I couldn't say with certainty that a train was or wasn't passing at that exact moment, I could say that I've never known it to cause anything in my condo to move before.

The Salt Lake City area that January, from the eleventh through the twenty-fifth, experienced a long cold spell; the average high temperature was twenty degrees with the average low thirteen degrees. That January was also the most humid month (with an average daily low humidity of 67 percent), the least windy month (with an average wind speed of five miles per hour), the month with the lowest cloud ceiling, and the month with the lowest visibility. These were favorable conditions for sound vibrations to travel, and although we can faintly hear the train horns, we've never felt them.

The last snowfall before the incident was 0.1 inch three days prior, and no snow had fallen during the week before that, so there were no snowplows out and about.

Hill Air Force Base was sixty miles from us, and we lived four miles, as the crow flies, from the Salt Lake International Airport, but we were not in the flight path of either. If any jets had broken the sound barrier, we would have heard a sonic boom. The Skypark Airport, which houses small private planes and a helicopter flight school, was four-tenths of a mile from us. While we did hear small planes and helicopters, especially in the summer, they did not fly nearby or overhead, and we were not aware of any air traffic that night.

Our condo was within a few miles of several oil refineries. On one occasion, a tank 2.2 miles from us exploded and caused our condo to shake, although nothing in the condo fell or noticeably moved. The explosion took place on the morning of August 30, 2012, four months before the flower-basket incident. I was upstairs in the master bathroom at the time, where I had a similar rectangular basket of greenery on top of a bathroom cabinet. That free-standing cabinet is against an outer wall with a window, which faced the direction of the blast. The window rattled, and I could feel the vibration under my feet, yet that basket didn't move or fall.

In spite of the industrial wasteland that it sounds like we inhabit, in the five years we've lived here, we've never seen or felt any movement, shaking, or vibration in the condo from garage doors, electrical appliances, traffic, snowplows, planes, trains, helicopters, or neighbors. The only time we've heard the windows rattle is when that tank exploded, or when there were extremely strong winds, which was not the case that evening.

Laurie said that things move naturally, just because of everyday vibrations within the house, such as opening and closing the refrigerator. Fair enough, but the basket isn't on top of the fridge. Might the repeated openings and closings of the door during the two weeks since I had dusted the basket have caused enough shake to make the basket descend? If that were the case, why in five years had similar action never triggered the basket to lean or fall? I could rule out opening and closing the cupboard below the basket and over the refrigerator, as I didn't use that cabinet. In fact, as I think of it now, I had no clue what's even in that cabinet, if anything. I could reach it only by climbing on a step stool.

Laurie said, "You need to determine the basket's center of gravity."

"What? How do I do that?"

"It takes a mathematical equation to figure it out."

Yeah. Like that's going to happen. If it ain't $x + y = z$, then my analysis would have to be incomplete here. Suffice it to say, the basket has had the same center of gravity for five years without tipping over, much less clearing the crown molding.

I had Jim get up on the step stool. He gave a slight tug on the front top of the basket to tip it forward so we could see how it would fall. The flowers came out of the basket and fell not onto the floor but onto the top of the refrigerator, which is directly below and extends eighteen inches beyond the cabinets. The flowers came to rest a good six inches from the front of the refrigerator—not even close to falling on the floor. The crown molding prevented the basket itself from tumbling. Had the flowers somehow cleared the refrigerator, they would have landed in front of the refrigerator, not three feet over to the stove where I stood at the time.

The only possible *physical* explanation for what happened was if the tops of the flowers had become off balance and leaned forward. They might have tipped forward, but they did not have enough weight to pull the basket over the crown molding with them. And if they had fallen on their own, the top of the refrigerator twenty inches below would have broken their fall, as there would be no force coming from behind them to push them farther. (Alas, Laurie, I did not calculate the mass, velocity, and momentum. I don't have a live-in physicist husband as you do, so you'll have to trust pure and simple logic on this one.)

So, is it a coincidence that the basket of flowers fell onto the floor and hit my leg on the night of my mother's eightieth birthday after I had asked for confirmation that she was with me? Possibly. But what are the odds? Besides, coincidence is just a convenient—not logical or scientific—so-called explanation.

After ruling out as many possible natural phenomena as I could, or, as scientists say, after falsifying the hypothesis—that is, the basket falling does not fit the known facts, and another theory or theories fit better—that leaves paranormal phenomena.

Something, or someone, had to push the basket from *behind* with enough force for it to hurdle the crown molding *and* the refrigerator to land feet away. Was it my mother? Was it someone acting on her behalf?

I couldn't say. But it was a memorable eightieth birthday in honor of my mother. That's indisputable. Now that I know she can move things, I hope it's just a matter of time before she can vacuum and dust my house.

CHAPTER 11

Are You Going to the Psychic Fair?

For a period of time, I experienced something paranormal nearly every day. One evening while Jim and I watched the news, Brian Williams announced that coming up next would be "the possible solution to one of the most enduring mysteries of the twentieth century." Jim asked me what I thought. Without thinking, I said Amelia Earhart. Sure enough, the segment told of a sonar image of what they thought might be her plane, the *Electra*, sunken off Howland Island.

As I drifted off to sleep each night, I saw in my mind's eye spirit faces and sometimes full-bodied people. I came to call them "spirits on parade." One night, they held a party. I could hear them laughing and conversing. It was so loud I woke up to tell them to take the party elsewhere. Another rule for my guides: I needed my sleep. Even though that's a time when the spirit world can more easily communicate with us, I told them, "No one interrupts my sleep unless they're friends or family."

Then some of my personal items started getting "misplaced." The pencil I keep on the end table by my recliner went missing. Normally, it's by the phone. I found it in the plastic basket I keep on the shelf of the end table. Not long after that, my lip balm went missing, which I keep in another plastic basket on the right side of my bathroom vanity. I found it in my right bathroom drawer. A few days later, when I reached for my toothbrush and toothpaste out of the other basket on the left side of my bathroom counter, I found my tube of eye cream. I keep that in the same basket with my lip balm. When my lip balm went missing again, I said aloud, "Okay. Who's messing with me? I love it, but where did you put my lip balm?" Without thought, I looked to my left, and there it sat next to my toothbrush. I am not this absentminded. Jim doesn't use my lip balm or my eye cream, and he knows better than to touch my pens and pencils. If I had been unconsciously moving things, I would think I'd have to hunt for them. All I had to do was ask, "Where is it?" and I'd be drawn right to it.

Then as quickly as all this phenomena began, it came to a halt. Days and weeks went by with nothing out of the ordinary happening. But I continued meditating, studying, and asking for confirmation from my guides. A few of my mediumship books talked about reaching a "plateau." Apparently, when you awaken your abilities, things speed along, but then you find yourself sitting alone on a spiritual mesa out in the middle of nowhere and feeling disconnected from your guides. I was about ten months into my journey when this happened. The books reassured that it wouldn't last. Why it happened, the books didn't say.

The books all suggested joining a development circle, as the vibrations and energy of others are contagious, which could spur a baby medium like me beyond this phase. I continued searching for one and found development classes on MeetUp.com only twelve miles from my home, but the woman who ran the classes had no credentials, such as certification from a Spiritualist church or any other certifying bodies. As a certified genealogist, I knew of many excellent genealogists not certified (Jim and my friend Dwight are two of them), but there were also plenty who had no clue how to do research.

Plus, we'd already had one bad experience with a noncertified medium. One of the local metaphysical stores held a psychic fair each month, which we discovered when we browsed the store one day. A flyer for a medium who looked to be in her early sixties drew my eye. Her picture looked, well, like any woman in her sixties with dyed hair. No tattoos. No piercings. No strands of crystals encircling her drooping neck. At home, I looked her up online and didn't find anything that turned me off. I hoped she'd be the real deal, as she offered development classes.

Since we'd never been to a psychic fair before, we weren't sure what to expect. Gypsies in glass booths with crystal balls? Men standing next to a large scale to guess our weight? Witches with tarot cards? Of course, it was nothing like that. Twenty-four women and men offered services ranging from aromatherapy to chakra balancing, from past life regressions to spiritual readings. The fair part was set up at the rear of the warehouse-style metaphysical store, separated by cloth dividers. The air smelled of incense, and the building was lit brightly with fluorescent lights. Many more customers patronized the store that day than when we had first visited. Some people browsed the Buddhas; others rubbed the crystals. We heard drums coming from a closed-off room where some sort of ceremony must have been taking place.

Jim had made back-to-back appointments for us through the online system, providing only our first names and his email address. Payment was to be made in cash when we arrived. Jim and I wore plain clothing so as not to give anything about ourselves away. He had on a teal sweatshirt with no lettering and jeans, and I wore an olive-green long-sleeved T-shirt and jeans. We wore no jewelry other than our claddaghs and wedding rings. The medium didn't see our rings, though, as we kept our hands in our laps under the card table where we sat with her.

The medium, who was dressed in a nondescript beige blouse and brown slacks, otherwise looked like her picture. Most women use photos of themselves when they were at least ten years younger. But she didn't. I liked that about her. She started by saying that she works with our spirit guides and gets messages from them. That was contrary to everything I'd ever read. Mediums do work with their own guides, but they bring through the spirits of our loved ones. She couldn't guarantee who would come though, she said. That wasn't surprising. She also told us she didn't want us to give her any information, which was good.

She read Jim first, and after bowing her head and sitting quietly for a few moments, she looked up and said she was getting a name like "Gerald." Jim has a dead uncle Gerard, and we both thought, *Wow, she's going to be good.* But it immediately went downhill from there.

She also received the name Shilling, which had no meaning for Jim, but she told him the year was 1892, and there was a grandfather and grandmother who lived close to the mountains. Now Jim became excited again. His paternal grandparents had lived in the Ozarks mountains. But then she said they lived "on the benches," which is a local term for the lower elevations of the Utah mountains. They had cattle and horses, she said, and they came here more for the adventure than their Mormon religion. But, oh, what a hard life they had! They weren't prepared for the weather conditions here, she said. There was a lot of anger and sadness. The six children eventually all left Utah and scattered to places like Oregon and California.

Let me pause here to explain something about one of the beliefs of the Church of Jesus Christ of Latter-day Saints. They believe in posthumous baptism by proxy. A living member of the church stands in for a deceased ancestor, and the ancestor is baptized into the LDS faith. The ancestor has free will and can accept or reject the baptism. I doubt seriously that Jim's Irish-American uncle Gerard—or Father Rowan, as his Minnesotan Catholic parishioners knew him—jumped at the chance to convert in the afterlife to the LDS faith when given the opportunity, and instead of his spirit progressing forward, he went back in time as Gerald Shilling, married, had six kids, and became a Utah pioneer.

When my turn came, I realized this was going to be more for entertainment than anything, so I had no expectations, only curiosity. The ancestor who came through for me, the medium said, was Charlene Taylor or Tyler, a woman in her late thirties or early forties and the first of five wives! She had three children, two boys and a girl. She was the wife who looked after and taught all the children in the family, and she made them aware of other religions and cultures, too, because she wanted to prepare them for their LDS missions.

The "medium" couldn't have been further from the truth had she told me I descended from Kunta Kinte. My ancestors were Italian-Irish Catholics with a dose of English and Scotch-Irish Protestantism who settled in New York, Connecticut, and Virginia. Jim's Irish and English ancestors settled in Minnesota and Arkansas. None of our ancestors were Mormon, and neither were we. Both of us are professional genealogists, so unless we've been tracing the wrong ancestors for the past thirty years, we're quite confident about their identities. Not to mention, we were the first in our families to move to Utah.

The poor dear (the medium, I mean) looked like she really struggled at various times. I felt bad for her. She sincerely believed she was a medium. We just smiled and nodded when she gave the "evidence," never asking us after each piece of information whether any of it rang true. So, I nearly choked on my own saliva when she finally asked Jim if any of the information from the reading made sense. Universe love him, he stumbled for a moment and said, "Well, some of it." We probably didn't do her any favors. She really did need to know how wrong she was. But we kept quiet.

At one point during the reading for me, I pleaded with spirit to put her (and us) out of her misery because she had so much trouble trying to remember her Utah pioneer history.

"That's all I'm getting," she finally said with a sigh of defeat after less than thirty minutes between the two of us. We'd paid for an hour.

I nodded in sympathy. "Do I go to the cashier to get a refund on the other thirty minutes?"

About six months into my journey, I joined a national organization called the Forever Family Foundation (or FFF) established in 2004. Part of their mission is to "establish the existence of the continuity of the family, even though a member has left the physical world, to stimulate thought among the curious, those questioning their relationship to the universe, and people who are looking for explanations of certain phenomena, and to financially support the continued research into survival of consciousness and Afterlife Science." On their scientific board were fifteen medical doctors and PhDs. They also certify mediums through a rigorous process. During these sessions, mediums seeking certification are required to provide a series of readings to different sitters. The information provided by the mediums is scored by the sitters utilizing a method devised by the foundation. In order to pass this certification, a medium must demonstrate composite scores that indicate significant proficiency, providing percentages of accuracy that are way beyond the statistical probability of chance.

The foundation created this program to help protect the public from frauds and from mediums not yet ready for prime time. According to co-founder Robert Ginsberg, for every twenty applications they send to those who inquire about certification, only one will come back to them. Of those who do apply, just 5 to 10 percent will become certified. At that time, there were twenty-eight certified mediums, including Theresa Captuo, of *The Long Island Medium*, and Kim Russo, host of *The Haunting of . . .*, a documentary-style television show with celebrities who share their paranormal experiences while Kim helps them make sense of them.

When the new member packet and current newsletter arrived, I set it aside and hadn't looked at it. But an email from the organization a month later caught my attention. The FFF annual conference, to be held in San Diego in November, was called "In Search of the Afterlife: Experiencing, Communicating & Connecting to Another World." Kim Russo would be the banquet speaker. Even though Theresa Caputo had inspired me to start this journey, the abilities Kim demonstrated on her show were even more impressive and later validated through research about the spirits she communicated with. She was certified not only by the foundation but also by the Windbridge Institute for Applied Research in Human Potential as a certified research medium.

The two-and-a-half-day conference consisted of presentations by scientists and certified mediums. As I read the topics, such as "The Role of the Brain in Receiving Communication," and saw there would be a scientific panel and demonstrations of spirit communication by several certified mediums, I became more excited. This might just be what the spirit doctor ordered. I shared it all with Jim, and that same day, we decided we'd go.

CHAPTER 12

Mom Pays a Visit

Two weeks after what would have been my mom's eightieth birthday (and the night I believed she knocked down my geranium flower basket), she visited me in a dream. My books on spirit communication agreed that when you have a vivid, logical, and memorable dream of someone who has passed, that's considered a spirit visitation.

On my mother's death certificate, it said she died from "anemia," but I never believed that. A few days before she died, Mom had stomach pain, her stools were black and tarry, and she vomited what medical personnel call "coffee grounds." All symptoms of internal bleeding. She bled to death internally, and I don't think it was a "coincidence" that my mom's doctor conveniently left town right after my mom died.

Not long before these symptoms appeared, her doctor had taken her off the blood thinner Coumadin and placed her on a new drug called Pradaxa, which has since been the subject of class-action lawsuits. I knew about the switch in meds but did not take the time to look up anything about the drug. I kick myself to this day. I discovered much too late that, in my mother's case, she had every condition listed as being contraindicated with the drug's usage.

Along with my guilt for not being more proactive in my mother's health care, I was also saddened that I had never gotten a chance to say goodbye to her. But all that changed the night my mother paid me a visit in my dream. Normally when I wake up, my sleep is a complete blank, as if someone has erased the blackboard of my mind, but this time, I recalled the dream with clarity:

I visited my mom in the nursing home where she resided.

"My stomach hurts," she said. "My stomachache is getting worse." Then, as if she were stating it would rain today, she said to me, "I'm dying."

There was no fear in her voice, and also no pain, which surprised me.

I hugged her and told her I loved her.

Even though I had always said, "I love you" to her when I talked with her, it wasn't until the last two or three years of her life that I came to appreciate my mother a little and actually like her. Dwight had suggested I read Bryon Katie's *Loving What Is*, and it helped me to change my attitude toward my mother. We snipped at each other a little less; instead, we good-naturedly teased one another. Our relationship slowly became more relaxed and comfortable. We got along fine when we gossiped about others in the nursing home, talked about our soap operas, or watched a chick flick together. With the burden off me for her care, and when she finally accepted that it was unrealistic to think that I could take care of her at home in her old age without killing her (on purpose), we relaxed and had a less cantankerous relationship.

At my mother's memorial service, I also saw another side to my mother. I saw her through the eyes of people who weren't her daughter, people who appreciated her and laughed with her. Growing up, I'd considered my mother deeply flawed: weak, insecure, and passive. Things I never wanted to be.

All things considered, I really wasn't a terribly troublesome daughter, or so I thought. I didn't do drugs, I didn't hang out with the wrong crowd, and I never got arrested. By the time I turned sixteen, I wanted to be independent and free from my mother's watchful eye. I was sexually active—never mind that she had had sex with my father before they married—and I was responsible enough to go to Planned

Parenthood for birth control. Of course, she had been a teenager in the conservative 1940s and 1950s. My teenage years came during the seventies' sexual revolution. I had never considered her a good mother, one whom I could go to for advice on problems, especially relationship problems. I agonized every Mother's Day to find an unsentimental card. My born-again Christian friend lifted my load somewhat when she told me, "The Bible doesn't say you have to love your parents. It says only that you have to honor them." But I wasn't even good at that when it came to my mother.

When Jim gave the eulogy at her memorial in the nursing home community room packed with staff and residents in wheelchairs and walkers, most with oxygen cannulas in their noses, for the first time, I saw my mother as a single parent with an untamable teenager. Although my father had left her, she should have left him. He was emotionally abusive. No wonder she had checked out of reality and suffered from bouts of severe depression. But she never gave up. She always had employment, always paid the bills, and always provided for me.

In actuality, my mom exhibited as a strong, independent, and caring person, not the weak individual I had painted her to be in my mind. It seemed difficult for her to express her caring, though, in any other way than telling me what to do. Then again, I fought her every step of the way. I shied away from her hugs, kisses, or any kind of affection from her. I pushed her away, as if she didn't matter, all because she hadn't lived up to my expectations of a mom, the kind of mom I saw on TV growing up: Donna Reed in the *Donna Reed Show* and Margaret Anderson in *Father Knows Best*. Heck, I would have settled for Morticia Addams as my mom. But I got Edith Bunker from *All in the Family*, a nervous woman who I thought couldn't stand up for herself.

As a preteen and teen, during the few times I had tried to confide in her my fears and deepest feelings, she would either tell me what I should do or she brushed aside my feelings with a positive spin as if *I* didn't matter. Sometimes positivity can be toxic, I heard on a TV show, when it ignores or denies the feelings and reality of a person. The blame wasn't entirely hers, though; much of it rested on my own shoulders. I could see that as my journey progressed. Sometimes it's not a straight line from here to there. As I was learning throughout this quest to become a medium, there were many unexpected detours.

In this dream, not quite two years after her death, I said to my mom, "I know my actions haven't always shown it, but I do love you."

Then I said to her something I had never, ever thought to say while she was alive: "You were a good mom. You did what you thought was best. The problem was I wasn't a good daughter."

On waking, I couldn't remember her reaction, but I remember that she then lay down on a couch and peacefully died.

Through this dream, or spirit visitation, my mother had given me the opportunity to say goodbye and to say what I wouldn't have been able to say at her deathbed. I finally took responsibility for my share of the conflict in our relationship.

Of course, my logical, skeptical mind would say that the detail of my mother complaining of a stomachache was nothing startling, since she bled in her stomach. It's an indisputable fact that she would have had stomach pain. When I reviewed the dream, that's really the only detail my mother gave me, other than to tell me she was dying, which I also knew. The dream could have been my subconscious at work, playing out unfinished business I had with my mother, but why nearly two years later? The dream was too real, too plausible. Dreams are rarely that.

When I awoke, I mourned my mother's passing all over again, but I also experienced a sense of peace and some closure, as if the chapter of turmoil in both of our journeys had ended. When I've said to people that I get along better with my mom now that's she dead, they think I'm being funny. Or morbid. I'm not.

While she was alive, even though our relationship had improved, I wasn't ready to accept more of the responsibility for my role in our troubled relationship. I was too absorbed in my feelings of hurt and disappointment that she wasn't the mother I had wanted her to be while I grew up. I resented too much in the later years that I had to disrupt my holidays and travel to see her. After the dream, it saddened me that we couldn't have achieved a more positive relationship while she was alive, and I felt guilty that I hadn't been a more patient and loving daughter. But then I realized this sadness and guilt were no longer necessary. This understanding and healing wasn't meant to happen while she was still alive. It was meant to come after she passed into spirit, when my heart and soul were open and ready for it.

My mother never lost her faith, even though she never returned to the Catholic Church, mostly because there was no Catholic church in the town where we'd last lived and where the nursing home was located. The priest from the neighboring town came to visit her. She belonged to a minority religion in the nursing home in that Evangelical Christian town, so he didn't come often. Each time he did, my mother mentioned it to me, and I'd ask, "Did he give you last rites?" She'd laugh and say no, but as infrequently as he visited, it wouldn't have been a bad precaution.

"I had him give me only half a communion wafer," she told me one time.

"Why? Are you on a diet?"

After Mom died, Brenda, the nursing home director, told me that every day my mother would stop her wheelchair halfway between the dining area and her room. There hung a wheelchair-height posting of the twenty-third Psalm, which my mom recited reverently and quietly, her lips moving. Even though I didn't believe in her God, I now saw a woman whose faith never wavered. I believed she met with the God of her understanding when she crossed. When people of all faiths, even atheists, have near-death experiences, they talk about seeing "white light" or "God." I now think that this Divine Whatever It Must Be manifests itself as the image a person would recognize from their own belief system. It makes sense why people needed to create a God in their own human image. It's harder to have a personal relationship with an abstract divine being, one that is pure energy and love. That's probably why Spiritualists were so fond of chumming up to their spirit guides; they had once lived in human form.

Another thing I've discovered is it's never too late to heal the wounds with deceased loved ones. My mother gave me a precious gift with that visitation. In spirit, I believe she wanted and needed the healing as much as I did here in the physical world, so we could both move on with our spiritual growth and journeys. This is why I can say in all honesty and seriousness that my mom and I now have a fantastic relationship.

CHAPTER 13

Las Vegas Getaway

Eleven months into my quest, Jim and I headed to Las Vegas for a weekend getaway for my fifty-seventh birthday. But it wasn't the glitz, glamour, or gambling that beckoned us. It was two Spiritualist churches. At the Spiritualist Desert Church, a guest Spiritualist medium, Rev. Karen, visited from Florida. We'd be attending her "message circle séance" on Saturday evening, then attending the Sunday morning service at the other church, the Spiritualist Church of Eternal Light. I couldn't remember the last time I had not only spent that much time in a church but looked forward to it. Oh, wait. Yes, now I remember. *Nev-er.*

We had lost our Spiritualist church virginity two months earlier when we visited Laurie in Oregon. The Alice Street Spiritualist Church in Portland was an hour away from Laurie's. She even agreed to go with us (if we bought her dinner), but the whole experience was disappointing. The evening service took place in the basement of the church president's home (that should have been our first red flag). The guest speaker wasn't a medium—she was an intuitive specializing in energy work. More than fifty of us packed into the basement on a balmy summer's night with no open windows, no air-conditioning, and no ventilation. It reminded me of my ancestors' journey to America, crammed into the steerage compartment of a ship. The intuitive's prophecies were interesting, but when she claimed she spoke to aliens, I rolled my eyes and thought, *Oh, geez. This is great. This is exactly what I wanted Laurie to hear.* There were no messages from the departed, traditionally a part of a Spiritualist service. We left an hour and a half later, sweaty, thirsty, and with no evidence for the afterlife.

On the way home, with Laurie in the back seat and a captive audience, Jim and I took the opportunity to discuss (badger) how the soul continues after death and there was science to back it up. Laurie probably felt like an animal with its foot caught in a steel-jawed trap, ready to gnaw off her own leg to get free from us.

"I wish I could believe," she said. "But I just can't."

Once we decided to go to Vegas and also to the Forever Family Afterlife conference in San Diego, I asked spirit to help us make some local contacts. Perhaps someone would have a like-minded relative or friend in Salt Lake City, or they could recommend a development circle. Before Jim and I headed out for our hot date in Vegas—a prime rib dinner and a séance—we meditated for ten minutes. I asked again for help finding a contact, and we each invited all our friends and loved ones who'd passed into spirit to attend the séance and church services. I knew they wouldn't all be able to give us messages, but I hoped we'd get specific details to validate they were with us. I had a small pool of dead people close to me. Sure, I have tons of ancestors and dead relatives (grandparents, aunts, and uncles), but unless I received verifiable information (not personality characteristics), I wouldn't recognize them.

We weren't sure about the appropriate attire for a séance, but whatever Jim and I wore, it had to give nothing away about us. We wanted to ensure that the medium wasn't doing a cold reading. I wore a green crewneck top with nice jeans, and Jim wore a blue golf shirt with slacks. Except for our rings, we wore no jewelry. Although Jim had tried calling the week prior to see if we needed to make reservations, he gave only his first name and his cell phone number. They never called us back, and we learned later that they hadn't received the message. My name is all over the internet, so I reminded Jim that if we had to sign a register, we'd sign it on the way out.

The Spiritualist Desert Church met in a small office in a strip mall. As we walked toward the building from where we parked, we heard a smoke alarm going off in one of the adjacent buildings. Once inside the church, I still heard the alarm, but no one else seemed bothered by it. I found it distracting and wondered how the medium would be able to concentrate.

Never having been to a real séance, Jim and I had no idea what to expect, except what we'd seen in movies and photographs on the internet. Madame Arcati in *Blithe Spirit* came to mind. In the play and the movie, Madame Arcati is a Spiritualist medium who conducts a séance for a writer suffering from writer's block. As everyone sits around a table holding hands, she accidentally conjures the spirit of the writer's deceased first wife, and that leads to an unexpected love triangle involving his current wife. Or maybe it would be like *Topper*, and we'd go home with a married couple in spirit who'd died in a car crash along with their ghostly St. Bernard dog to annoy and watch over us.

In the church, folding chairs had been arranged in a circle, and about half a dozen people sat chatting with each other. The church space was sparsely decorated with framed paintings of landscapes and angels. At the entrance stood a lectern, and a woman behind it took the fee for the séance as people arrived. I didn't know whether she was the guest medium. She was a heavyset woman with swollen calves and ankles who wore a dusty purple dress with sequins, dark-purple shoes with sequins, and a purple hat with netting. She actually could have been Madame Acarti. As it turned out, she was one of the church's board members. Everyone else dressed casually, so we hadn't underdressed or overdressed. Eventually, there were twelve of us, Jim and I included, nine women and three men. Almost all were about our age, in their fifties and sixties, with a few young women in their thirties. One older man was alone, the other with, we presumed, his wife.

Many greeted us, and although we tried to be incognito and not give away information about ourselves, we had to make small talk and answer questions such as whether we lived in Vegas. That turned out to be a good thing, because when we said we lived in Salt Lake City, a couple of church members told us about three other members who also lived in Salt Lake. They couldn't remember their names, unfortunately, since they didn't come often.

The minister, a woman in her sixties dressed plainly in a button-down shirt and slacks and with close-cropped graying hair, arrived along with the guest medium, Rev. Karen. She was a certified medium through the National Association of Spiritualist Churches and an ordained minister. Fit and trim, Rev. Karen was an attractive blonde in her mid-fifties with shoulder-length hair. She wore a long, royal-blue skirt and a matching blouse with a print in royal blue, green, and black.

Before things started, Jim went up to her and asked if she allowed taping, but she said no. She encouraged us to take notes, however. We planned that when Jim received his reading, I would take notes, and when I received mine, he would take them, so we could record everything in real time and not rely on memory later.

The lights remained on—I later saw a bumper sticker that read, SPIRITUALISTS DO IT WITH THE LIGHTS ON. We didn't hold hands, and no candles burned. I didn't even smell any sage. The "message circle séance" was what might be called a group reading. When Rev. Karen began, she stood at the front of the room, closed her eyes, and muttered to herself—or rather, to spirit. She opened her eyes, then moved to stand directly in front of the person she wanted to deliver the message to. She smiled at the person and said hello. She closed her eyes again and kept them closed throughout the reading.

Occasionally, she opened her eyes, asked if the person understood the message, then she closed them again and continued. She waved her arms around a lot and used a lot of hand gestures. Maybe the spirit person was deaf, and she needed to use sign language. During one reading, she said she smelled something but could only get a whiff of it. She kept moving her hand up toward her nose, like she was trying to get the smell back.

When someone from the person's mother's side came through, she motioned to the right; for the father's side, to the left. She said when someone stood behind another person, that, for her, meant it was the next generation back. When the spirit stood further away, that meant an aunt or uncle or someone more distantly removed. My mediumship books had mentioned working out a system with your spirit guides, so this all made sense to me.

Everyone received a message, each about ten minutes long, and no two readings were alike in any way, except when she told the person she read that the spirit was a mother figure, father figure, grandmother figure, and so on. One lady received a message from a woman who liked to sew. I hadn't received my message yet, and I kept thinking, *No, no. That message must be for me. It's my mom.* My mother had been a professional seamstress and worked for a dry cleaner. She made all of my clothes and my dolls' clothes. My mother also knitted, but she never did any other kind of needlework, like cross-stitch or tatting. The more details Rev. Karen gave, it became clear it was not the type of sewing my mother did.

"She did some kind of close stitching and needed glasses when she sewed," Rev. Karen told the woman. My mom did wear glasses, but the close stitching she described sounded like needlework. Rev. Karen never said that the woman was a seamstress.

"She would have liked to do sewing for work, but she did it for herself," Rev. Karen said. That definitely was not my mother.

Even though Rev. Karen kept her eyes closed and received no visual clues about whether she was correct or not, the woman receiving this message smiled and nodded all through it.

The woman I sat next to and had met before the circle began hailed from the Cotswolds in England. She was raised a Spiritualist. During her reading, Rev. Karen rolled her hands together: "She's making meatballs or something." After the séance, I asked the lady about that and whether it was accurate. "Oh, yes!" she said. "That was my grandmother. She was a Spiritualist, and she always comes through in messages. What she was shaping with her hands was dumplings. My grandmother always made dumplings."

I'd read that messages can't be taken too literally because each medium filters what she's getting through her own mind and frame of reference. If I saw a vision of a woman shaping something circular with her hands, I would have assumed she made meatballs, too.

Rev. Karen, always with her eyes closed, would occasionally say aloud, but softly, "I don't understand. Say it again." And one time she said to an attendee, "I don't know why she's telling me this, but you get what I get."

About halfway into the evening, Rev. Karen approached Jim, smiled, said hello, asked how he was doing, then closed her eyes. (The italics below represent our interpretation of the readings after they occurred.)

"A gentleman has stepped in with you. He's a father figure." *Probably Jim's dad.*

"He was in some form of the service." *Jim's dad was in the Army for ten years from 1936 to 1946, but having served would be true of most men of that generation.*

"He's taller than I am, of average build." *Correct.*

"I see a picture of him when he was younger; he has a hat on." *Jim didn't know of any picture of his dad with a hat on.* "I can see sideburns and hair." *Again, this didn't sound familiar to Jim.*

"He has similar features to you, but there's a difference in the cheekbones in this picture." *If it was the picture Jim was thinking of when Jim's dad was younger, this was correct.*

"I smell smoke." *Here is where I wanted to say, "It's probably us. We just came from the casino where we had our prime rib dinner," but I refrained.* "He was a smoker at this time in life." *Jim's dad smoked cigars, something I didn't know.*

"He was a leader of people." *Jim's dad was a first sergeant at Fort Snelling, Minnesota, and a tank commander during World War II.*

"There were groups of people he interacted with." *True, in the Army, but also a vague detail.*

"He was very smart." *Yes.* "He liked to put things together." *Yes.*

While the information could be considered generic, it does mostly fit Jim's dad. When I compared the same details to my father, for example, most of the information does not fit. Interestingly, Rev. Karen didn't give anyone else a message of a father being in the military, even though it probably fit for the majority of attendees.

Rev. Karen continued. "There's a lady figure stepping in. It's his mother." *She meant his father's mother, Jim's paternal grandmother, Roxanna.*

"She went to the spirit world when you were younger." *True. Jim was sixteen, a sophomore in high school.*

"They've both been around you and watching 'things spin,' but it's okay to stop the wheel. They're trying to help you. It's about something financial." *Suffice it to say that this message was spot on. For the first time, Jim realized that it wasn't just people we knew well who watched over us but our ancestors, too. Jim had only met this grandmother once, when he was five.*

"There's another gentleman vibration stepping in," said Rev. Karen. "He's a generation out. It feels like an uncle vibration." *Possibly Jim's maternal uncle Gerard, the Catholic priest, and with whom Jim was close.*

"He lived in the east. I mean east of here, but not on the East Coast." *Father Gerard lived in Minnesota.*

"There's a book of his he handed down in the family."

Jim and I both later told each other that we were thinking of a genealogy book or family history, but she never said that, so she wasn't reading our minds.

"It's a technical book that's been passed down in the family." *While genealogy is not technical to us, it might be to someone not familiar with it. Jim has some of Father Gerard's books and notebooks from the seminary on various topics, including cosmology, that Jim would consider technical. Plus, Father Gerard handed down his journals.*

"There's going to be a celebration around August 17 or 18," said

Rev. Karen. *This date had no significance for Jim or me.* "Something will happen around that time, and they'll all be with you."

"The lady is blowing you a kiss. I will leave her with you and love and blessings."

A few people later, it was my turn. I had expected her to come to me last, so when she stood in front of me and said, "You knew I was coming to you next." I thought, *Actually, no, I didn't know that.*

Like with everyone else, as she stood in front of me, she kept her eyes closed during my entire reading.

"A lady has stepped forward for you." *Rev. Karen gave no indication of the relation.* "She had great love for family." *At the time, this felt too generic and didn't click with me. Later, when I figured out the spirit was my friend Marsha Rising, I felt "family" could be symbolic for the genealogy family Marsha and I had been part of when she was alive.*

"She was happy just to have snacks or tea and crumpets with people." *Hold the phone! Now I wondered if the message was for the English lady sitting next to me. I didn't know anyone who had tea and crumpets. Marsha didn't snack. But she did drink tea, and she loved to have meals with everyone.*

Rev. Karen continued, "She was very friendly, easy to talk to, no matter what was going on." *This definitely described Marsha. Before she became a full-time genealogist, she was a social worker. In our genealogy family, she was like our den mother, and the one everyone sought for advice. She loved helping people with their problems, whether genealogical or personal.*

"She's with two other ladies." *This is when I knew it must be Marsha. Two of our genealogy family had died around the same time as Marsha. Sandra Leubking, a good friend of Marsha's, died a year to the day after Marsha and of the same type of ovarian cancer. The other friend, Birdie Holsclaw, died three months after Marsha of breast cancer.*

"They are like the Three Musketeers. They do things together." *This made sense. It wouldn't surprise me that they'd all find each other in the spirit world and were busy tracking down their ancestors.*

"She had a moderate build, was a little taller than me." *True.*

"I see her sitting at a kitchen table, covered with laminate, with metal trim and legs. She's drinking tea and looking out the window in the early morning. That was her time alone before everyone else was up." *Not likely. Marsha was not an early riser, but, again, she did drink tea. The table, which sounded like a 1950s kitchen table, was nothing like the glass table in Marsha's kitchen.*

"She's showing me a bracelet, tucked in a jewelry box." *Rev. Karen was insistent about this—or the spirit was. She kept encircling her wrist with the other hand. I didn't recall Marsha ever wearing a bracelet, and even though I have four or five bracelets, I rarely wear them, but they are tucked in my jewelry box. Marsha never gave me a bracelet.*

"She's saying there's been some distance between you and your family members, but to keep the heart connection. She says she understands now why there's been the distance." *I assumed she meant the distance between me and my deceased mother.*

"There's another lady, a friend of hers." *I couldn't tell whether this was Sandra or Birdie or someone else. It sounded as if it was another friend, though.* "There was a game they used to play with cards. It wasn't solitaire or blackjack." Rev. Karen opened her eyes and said to me that those were the only types of card games she knew. *Marsha played Spider Solitaire on her computer, and I knew her husband played bridge, but I didn't think Marsha had.* Then Rev. Karen closed her eyes again. "This other lady said that you're playing the right cards, that you've done that so far, and to keep going as you have been. This is why you haven't made the move yet." *I had been thinking about going back to school to get additional English credits or a PhD, but I hadn't made a move yet.*

But there was something else to keep in mind: Rev. Karen's accuracy rate and my attempt at interpreting what she received. "Even the best reader, psychic, or shaman," notes Ann Marie Chiasson, MD, in *Energy Healing*, "accurately interprets the meaning of a vibration only 80 percent of the time. The images, vibrations, and feelings are always correct, yet we get caught in our own material when trying to discern their meanings."

Then Rev. Karen said to me, "I have another woman stepping in." *Again, she didn't give a relationship to me. It was like a guessing game.* "She's shorter, five foot one or two." *This could be my dad's mom, the only grandparent I knew, or my mom, as she had shrunk from osteoporosis.*

"The woman is bent over." *Definitely not my grandmother. She had perfect posture even on her deathbed. Still could be my mom.*

"She had white curly hair." *My mom had faded strawberry-blond, curly hair.*

"Her face is smooth, not a lot of wrinkles." *No, not my mom.*

"She was eighty-two, eighty-four when she died." *My mom was seventy-eight when she died. I had no clue who this was.*

"She worked in the garden. I can see flowers." *Not anyone I knew.*

"But I'm also seeing some kind of vegetables, but I can't tell what they were. I can see only the tops of them. She's said that it looks like the plants aren't doing well, like they won't survive the first year, but next year they will bear fruit. So, you should hang in there. Trust the process. I leave her with you with love and blessings." *My friend Dwight has always told me to "trust the process." He said it to me on our second research trip to Ireland, when I went through some difficult times. Rev. Karen did not say these words to anyone else during the evening. The symbolism of the message certainly resonated with me. I'd been wondering why I've been going through bouts where I don't feel as connected to spirit. I was now eleven months into my journey and wasn't feeling like this project was going well. But I also knew I would "hang in there," and this could be a reminder to "trust the process."*

It bugged me that I couldn't figure out the identity of this spirit, though. When I told Dwight about it, he said the message is more important than the messenger, but I didn't agree. If someone I had little respect for gave me a message like this, I wouldn't give it any special credence; but if it's someone important to me, the message would hold a great deal of significance.

On the car ride home, as I transcribed our notes into my laptop, Jim and I talked about the messages we received. He said, "Read back the details about the woman who said 'Trust the process.'" As I read through each detail, he said, "That sounds like my mom."

"How old was she when she died? Rev. Karen said she was between eighty-two and eighty-four. That doesn't fit anyone I know."

"My mom was eighty-four."

Of course, Clare would say "trust the process" and would know it had special meaning for me. She was there in Ireland with me when Dwight had said it to me. On that trip, I first sensed her in the gift shop in Knock, and she had spoken to me at Carrabba's. Why she would take the opportunity to give me a message and not Jim, though, puzzled me. I guess Clare knew I needed the communication more at this stage in my journey.

CHAPTER 14

Is My Aura on Straight?

The next morning, we attended the Spiritualist Church of Eternal Light, although we almost skipped it. We felt in sync with the Spiritualist Desert Church after the previous night's séance and the people we met there. When Jim and I read about the Church of Eternal Light online, we weren't too impressed with what we saw, but we were eager to receive more messages. I wanted to see if any of the same spirits would come through to validate our experience from the prior night.

Like the Desert Church, the Church of Eternal Light occupied office space in a strip mall, but in another part of town. This space was much larger than the other church, though, with fifty or more chairs in place. They faced a small, cloth-draped altar with candles and what looked to be a Christmas tree angel lit with fiber optics. In the corner to the right stood a lectern. A divider wall that didn't come full to the ceiling was decorated on top with various sizes and shapes of ceramic angels. A few looked like lawn ornaments.

When we entered, we noticed a table by the door with pamphlets, and Jim, without thinking, signed the register. He entered us as Jim and Sharon Warren of Salt Lake City, Utah. I didn't feel there was much harm after I noticed what he'd done, as I've never used the name Sharon Warren. A woman greeted us, then another, who introduced herself as Rev. Virginia. She was my height, thin, probably in her late seventies. Her matching teal suit and shoes contrasted with her short, loosely permed, dyed black hair. She welcomed us and asked our names. We said Jim and Sharon. She told us she was happy we came, then encouraged us to take a seat; the service would be starting soon.

Again, we had dressed plainly, Jim in a lavender golf shirt and me in a plain pink shirt, and no jewelry except for our rings. We took a seat in the second row on the left side facing the altar. Roughly thirty-six people attended, young and old alike, but no children.

Rev. Virginia opened the service with a meditation, then we sang a hymn called "I'm Not Gonna Worry," which had my name written all over it.

We then read in unison from I Corinthians 12:4–6 and a passage from the Aquarian Gospel, which I later learned had the actual title *The Aquarian Gospel of Jesus the Christ: The Philosophic and Practical Basis of the Religion of the Aquarian Age of the World and of the Church Universal*. It's a book published in 1908 by Levi H. Dowling that's been adopted by some New Age spiritual groups and is supposed to be a compendium of mystical knowledge. Then we read something from Kahlil Gibran, a Lebanese artist, poet, and writer, and sang another hymn, "Come Into the King's Chambers."

Between the readings and hymns, it was clear this was a Christian Spiritualist church. When the guest speaker, Rev. Pam, gave her lecture, "When God Calls You, Listen," with numerous quotes from the Bible, it all seemed a little too religious and traditional for my liking. One unconventional aspect was only women conducted the service. Pam, a short, obese woman who dressed in dark slacks, a white button-down shirt, and a sweater-vest, wore her hair cropped like a man. She used a cane, as she had recently had knee surgery. My Catholic upbringing was a little offended when I noticed she wore rosary beads as a necklace. Wasn't that like wearing the American flag? She had an East Coast accent, and I suspected she was raised Catholic, too. Maybe she had been a nun.

Announcements followed the offering, and Rev. Virginia, even with notes in front of her, had some problem keeping them straight. She announced that another minister of the church, Rev. Alice, was leaving. A huge gasp of shock reverberated throughout the congregation. She also announced a guest medium would visit from Spain at the end of the month, David Darnbrough.

Rev. Alice guided us in mediation. She had us sit with our eyes closed and palms facing up on our thighs. New Age music played, then she sped us through the quickest meditation I'd ever experienced. (As quick as it takes you to read this is as long as the meditation lasted.) She asked us to envision a green light at our feet and to move it up our bodies. I still had the green light at my calves when she moved on to seeing a light in a silver tunnel that we were supposed to walk (run?) through. In the tunnel, she said, were sparkling silver lights, and at the end was a large amethyst. Rev. Alice had some problems pronouncing "amethyst." It came out as "amthist." We were to be around the amethyst, but we mustn't dally long (my words), as then we would see an emerald-green light. I had just barely made the visual transition when Rev. Alice asked us to visualize three gold circles, one for the Father, one for the Mother, and one for our consciousness. She left us in peace with the trinity for a second or so, then she guided us back to the real world.

After a healing session, then came the part Jim and I were here for: the message service. Members from the congregation—mediums in training—came up one by one to give two or three readings each. They each picked someone in advance, apparently at random, then asked before each reading, "May I bring you a message?" No one said, "No," but I would have liked to see what they would have done with that response.

One woman, who looked in her forties, was dressed in black slacks and wore a yellow top, with a pretty yellow-and-orange sheer blouse. Before each reading, she stood with her eyes closed and palms up. When she opened her eyes, she had a clear fix on someone in the room. For whatever reason, I instantly liked her and hoped she'd give me a reading, but she didn't. Then again, the reading she gave one man didn't seem to resonate with him at all. She talked about a father figure, and that he was a coach who wore shorts. She asked the man if his father played basketball or football, but he said no. "He's coaching you from the sidelines," she said. She didn't seem flustered that the man didn't make a connection, and said, "That's what I'm getting."

Two other women gave readings, including Rev. Alice. It approached 1 p.m. (the service had begun at eleven), and when Rev. Virginia stood up, I assumed the service was over. I was disappointed that neither Jim nor I received messages. But then Rev. Virginia gave a reading to a man, and then she looked in my direction.

"May I give you a message?"

Because of the glare on her glasses, I couldn't tell whether she looked at me or the person behind me, so I said, "You mean me?"

Everyone laughed, and she said, "Yes, you!"

I laughed and said, "Yes, of course!"

"Sharon, right?" She had remembered my name from when we introduced ourselves. She said, "I'm seeing something I don't see very often. There's a gold aura around you. I've seen it before, but not often." I beamed, of course. "You have a lot of wisdom," she continued. "I don't know if you're a teacher, are you?"

I nodded that I was.

"Spirit has so much to bring through you."

Naturally, I was surprised and flattered. She had the teacher part right, but who can validate whether I have a gold aura around me or if it's even on straight? Later, I looked up what gold auras mean. One website said,

The color gold represents wisdom and knowledge from a higher source, a higher dimension. Persons who display this color within their human energy fields are accessing information from a higher level. They are highly intuitive at times, very perceptive, and possess a sense of heightened awareness. Gifted teachers and counselors are prime examples of people who have gold energy around them. This golden light is not always apparent within the auras of such people. It becomes more visible and amplifies in width and intensity when they teach and counsel others using their special psychic abilities.

Now I understood why I couldn't tell whether Rev. Virginia looked at me or not. My gold aura must've been reflecting off her glasses. I was rather surprised and disappointed that the congregation didn't immediately gather around me after the service, wanting to rub my head for good luck, or, at the very least, break out in the Hallelujah chorus, bow at my feet, and hail me as their new prophet.

I think the gold aura might have been my new hair color. It did have some gold highlights.

What Rev. Virginia said next blew Jim and me away. She said, "There's a female, and her name is Norma." (I have changed the name, but the real name is equally uncommon, ranking between seventy-five and one hundred of the top one hundred baby names for the decade of her birth.)

I could feel Jim practically come out of his seat, and I'm sure I looked surprised, too. The name took us completely off guard. We couldn't help but react. I nodded a confirmation. My brain scrambled to remember if I knew anyone else named Norma, besides Jim's ex-wife.

Pastor Virginia made it clear it was someone not in spirit but who was here in the physical world (true) when she said, "There have been difficulties between you both, but they were being wiped away. There is something that you hold that she will need."

Besides Jim? I thought.

"She seems to reach back out to you."

Of course, I understood the difficulties, but not only would hell have to freeze over, but birds would have to start meowing before Norma would be in touch with me about anything.

Jim and I said later that if this prediction came true, we'd move to Vegas, join that church, and take care of Rev. Virginia for the rest of her life.

Then Rev. Virginia said there was an elderly woman not in good health away somewhere. She said she was a small person, maybe about five feet. She asked for confirmation.

"No one is immediately coming to me," I said, "but I did have someone like that in spirit." But clearly, she wasn't talking about someone who'd passed. Later, I remembered my grandmother's cousin, Isabel, now in her nineties, was a small woman, barely five feet tall.

Rev. Virginia said there would be a document coming that I'd have to sign. She pointed to Jim and said, "But he won't agree with it. You should listen to him." Everyone laughed.

Bursting with excitement by the time we returned to our hotel room, I had to call Laurie to share the message. This would surely convince her. After I told her what had happened, I said, "What do you think?" She said she didn't know because she wasn't there, but "There's probably an explanation for it." When did my daughter become such a killjoy? I bet she goes to the county fair with a pin and pops little kids' balloons, right after she trips them. Laurie thought the minister probably Googled us.

"She wouldn't have had time. Besides, we didn't give her our last names when we introduced ourselves." I admitted that Jim had signed the register when we came in, which in hindsight was not the best thing to do. I suppose Rev. Virginia could have had an accomplice in the back room Googling everyone who came in, but that didn't seem likely. And to what end? Rev. Virginia had been an assistant pastor for five years at the other church we attended the previous night, then she founded this church thirteen years ago. I wouldn't call the good woman charismatic, and by no stretch of the imagination did she fit the profile of a cult leader. Considering many skeptics are eager to publicly discredit mediums, I didn't find anything negative online about Rev. Virginia or her church. Our only complaint was the church seemed too focused on traditional

Bible teachings and not enough on the principles of Spiritualism. The readings she did for me, however, I realized much later, were psychic. They didn't come from the spirit world.

After I hung up with Laurie, I Googled "Jim and Sharon Warren Salt Lake City," and emailed the results to Laurie. Our website came up, but my name was not listed anywhere as Sharon Warren, but as Sharon DeBartolo Carmack. Of course, if someone looked at our photo, they'd know it was us. Even if someone had Googled us, they'd be hard-pressed to find Jim's ex-wife's name, Norma. They'd been divorced for more than ten years. If you Googled just Jim Warren, pages of men by that name came up, and none of them were Jim. If you Googled Jim Warren and Salt Lake City, we're back to our website, which had no mention of Norma.

Laurie thought it was a lucky guess that she picked the name Norma. I had no doubt exasperation came through in my voice over the phone. "How many friggin' Normas do *you* know?"

Rev. Virginia didn't mention any other names to me, such as when she mentioned the short, elderly lady who wasn't well. It wasn't as if she hemmed and hawed, saying, "I'm getting a name with an N, it could be Nancy, Noelle, Norma . . ." Without uncertainty or hesitation, she said, "Norma." Out of the millions of names in the universe, how would she possibly guess the one name that we had a connection with?

But based on our reaction, Laurie tried to rationalize again, it probably gave the woman enough information to go on to say there had been difficulties between me and Norma. Come on. Really? Let's be logical about this. The reaction we had was certainly one of surprise, but that could mean anything. We would have shown equal surprise if she'd said "Laurie," or given us an uncommon name of a beloved family member or friend. Our surprised reaction meant only one thing to Rev. Virginia or to anyone else—she'd given us a name that had significance to us. Nothing more.

Even though I knew Laurie was a skeptic and we would never agree on the topic, it hurt that she wasn't more supportive, only critical of my experience. There had been plenty of instances in her life that I hadn't agreed with or approved of, but I don't recall ever being as disparaging as she was. Relief washed over me when she emailed:

I feel bad for shooting down your experience. I'm such a horrible daughter. I'm sorry. There's just so much that has accumulated to my current beliefs about the world. We're talking since high school! So, I'm sorry for being so skeptical. It's just unlikely that your one experience will change fifteen years of my own understanding of how the world works.

Yes, I, too, Googled you and Jim. Did you find JimAndSharonsAdventures? It's such a funny blog about a couple who bikes around the US. I didn't find any connections to you guys and Norma.

After the service, I thanked Rev. Virginia, and she gave me a hug. I told her that Norma was the name of Jim's ex-wife. This time, she looked surprised and said, "Oh my!" What did I deduce from her surprised reaction? She's either a good actress, or she's the real deal.

CHAPTER 15

The Afterlife Conference

No sooner had we returned from our Vegas pilgrimage when it was time to leave for the Forever Family Foundation Afterlife Conference in San Diego. I never knew what to expect when we attended these things. Everyone looked as if they belonged at a genealogical conference. Most of the hundred or so attendees were White, middle-aged or older, and female—Jim counted only seventeen men among the crowd—with one Black woman and several Hispanics and Asians. Except for the man with a shaved head and orange robes, anyone walking into the opening banquet would have no clue what type of conference this was. I wondered if anyone had prepared the waitstaff. What went through their minds when celebrity medium Kim Russo made her appearance after we ate and had us begin with a short meditation to ask our loved ones in spirit to join us?

When we arrived for the meet and greet before the banquet, we chatted with two women, who both looked to be in their sixties. One had been to every one of these conferences except one, and her friend was a first-timer like we were. They, too, found the science behind consciousness survival interesting and recommended I read books by physicists Claude Swanson and Amit Goswami, who, they said, made quantum physics understandable. I'll be the judge of that!

Jim and I found a table near the front of the room with six others, all women. The woman next to me said she took online parapsychology courses offered by one of the speakers, Loyd Auerbach, who earned his master's degree in parapsychology in the 1980s. She and her husband, who hadn't come to this conference, go on paranormal investigations when they travel. They look online for local ghost tours. That might be fun, but I knew these were generally held late at night.

"Why is all the ghost hunting done so late?" I asked her. "I can barely stay awake past nine."

"The earth is more quiet then. Most businesses and factories are closed, and most people are asleep. You become more sensitive to the spirit world's vibrations then."

She looked to be in her mid-forties, and I noticed she wore a cross and several small religious medals on a chain. When I asked her about these, she told us that her uncle was a priest who did exorcisms. "We have lively debates about all this. He thinks that anything paranormal is the work of the devil. I said to him, 'How can talking to my angels and loved ones be demonic?'"

"Why did he decide to become an exorcist?" I asked.

"You don't decide. You're chosen. He went to the Vatican for training."

She said every archdiocese now has a priest who can do exorcisms, but that it used to be there were only two in the country: one handled cases east of the Mississippi, the other handled the west. "I'm not sure why the church feels they need one in each archdiocese now, or why the need has increased."

After the meal, Kim Russo stood front and center, looking just as lovely as she did on television. A woman in her forties, I'd guess, she wore a fashionable, black, two-piece evening dress. Her dark-blond highlighted hair, slightly longer than shoulder length, appeared even prettier in person. She asked the audience how many had seen her show, *The Haunting of . . .* Many hands went up, but not as many as I expected. Jim and I had been watching her show since I happened upon it one night about six months into my journey. I blame her for getting me hooked on buying crystals.

Be forewarned: If you have the slightest tendency toward an addiction, stay away from crystals. With each show, Kim shared a different one. I then ordered each online, and soon I dragged Jim along with me to metaphysical shops and to the gem fairs held twice a year in search of more crystals. I collected more than two dozen different varieties in all shapes, sizes, and colors, in duplicates and octuplicates, and as wands, pendants, and bracelets, all of which were quite lovely and shiny. Each crystal was supposed to open something, close something, ward off something, connect with something, heal something, but mostly they just emptied something from my bank account and depleted something of Laurie's inheritance. ("You left me rocks?") The only thing I had ever collected before was dead relatives, and they didn't take up as much room. But Kim didn't wear any crystals tonight, unless she had them tucked in her bra.

Kim said that when the producer first approached her about doing the show, she hesitated because television has to make everything scary. (In the show's opening, which Kim narrates, she says the celebrity guest wants to go back to their "terrifying" paranormal experience. Most aren't the least bit terrifying.) The producers wanted that fear factor, but, Kim said, as she started doing the show, family members of the celebrities would come through with messages for them. In the end, the producers liked this aspect, so a portion of the show now dealt with the celebrities getting readings.

Kim explained what she's learned from being a psychic medium, as she calls herself, for the past eighteen years. When we cross to the other side, Kim said with her New York accent, no one judges us. But if we want to advance to the next level, we have to make our wrongs right, so many spirits are trying to do just that. We have to be open to the signs they're giving us and to trust the signs. They work hard to get us to notice them. But we must remember that the spirit world gives us what we need, not necessarily what we want.

She explained that their world mirrors our own world, but it's all in thought form. Language isn't needed on the other side. Everything is spoken through consciousness. They don't sleep, because there is no physical body that needs rejuvenation.

Our souls always have free will, she continued. You don't have to reincarnate unless you want to. The lessons we learn here in the physical world are hard. "I don't envy children being born now," she said, "because the lessons will be harder." Everything boils down to unity, love, and peace.

Then she explained how she works, as each medium works a bit differently. She's mostly clairvoyant and clairaudient. When she's talking with someone on the other side, the two questions she always asks are "Who are you? How did you pass?" to get validation. She often gets numbers, which are usually birthdays or passing dates.

"I have no control over who comes through," she said and smiled, adding, "I'm not Dial the Dead."

After the laughter died down, she began her readings, moving among the audience to where she felt drawn. The waitstaff had finished clearing, and the room fell silent, all of us hanging on her every word. Her high heels clicked across the linoleum floor, and she stopped behind us. She said she was getting the name "George." "Are you George?" she said to the gentleman she stopped at. The man said, "Yes." Everyone appeared stunned, of course, but then I realized we all had place cards at our tables with a colored dot to tell the waitstaff whether we were eating chicken or salmon. I flipped my place card upside down so my name wasn't visible. Jim did the same thing, then so did everyone else at the table. Guess we're all a bit of a skeptic at heart.

Actually, from where Kim stood a few feet away from the man, unless she had Superwoman eyesight, she couldn't have read the print on the three-by-five place card.

At one point, I thought she was going to come to me, but she didn't.

She stood near a table right behind us and to the left, a little more than arm's length away. As she wrapped up her reading there with two gay men, she said a couple of times that she felt drawn behind her, that something was pulling her behind her. I hoped she was coming to me.

When she turned around, she asked, "Who connects with the name 'Madeline' or some other 'Ma' name?"

I said, "Marsha?"

As she walked past me, she said, "No, it's not Marsha, it's Madeline or . . ."

At that point, it wouldn't be my lucky night or Jim's.

A young woman at our table did get a reading, and then the next day during the conference, that same woman received another reading from one of the other mediums, and she won a door prize! When we next saw her, we told her we needed to sit by her for the rest of the conference. Then on the last day, the woman won yet another door prize! Geez. Talk about having good spirit guides.

The next morning, the banquet room had undergone a transformation with the round dining tables removed and long, narrow tables in their place. We sat toward the back; then the row in front of us began filling with all the mediums, including Kim Russo.

The program over the next two days alternated between presentations by various scientists and demonstrations by certified mediums. Loyd Auerbach, the one who offered the online courses in parapsychology, kicked off the first day, saying many people have had paranormal experiences, but they refuse to accept it or talk about it. He said that when he opens the door by talking about the paranormal, many people will confide in him, saying, "I've never told anyone this, but . . ." He said people will tell him that they are sure there was a spirit in the room with them, but they didn't know who it was. He'll say, "Did you ask? If you don't know who the ghost is, ask them! They're people, too."

Loyd added that one of the first things science has to do is "reach a definition of consciousness. I don't think we'll get mainstream science to accept that there is an afterlife unless they conclude that there is something to survive."

Janet Mayer, a certified research medium and author of *Spirits . . . They Are Present*, shared her unusual journey. A petite, outgoing woman with thick, long, brunette hair, Janet explained how she had attended a spiritual retreat and walked away spontaneously speaking a foreign language that she'd never spoken before, nor did she know what she said.

"Many people offered guesses as to what the language was," she told the audience, "but no one could identify the origin." She began an exhaustive search to try and solve the mystery. "I spent the next four and a half years mailing cassette tapes around the country, trying to find someone who could tell me what I was speaking. I couldn't explain how, but I knew that this was a true language; someone was trying to get a message across.

"I was blessed to find a man named Ipupiara," she continued, "who worked at the Smithsonian Institute. He was able to translate my language." As it turned out, the language was one from an indigenous people living in a tropical rain forest of northern Brazil and southern Venezuela in South America. Known as the Yanomami, the tribe had no contact with the outside world until the mid-1950s. "They believe that their fate is tied to the fate of our environment," Janet said.

She then explained that "after receiving the translation of many of my tapes, I have discovered that I am speaking prayers, ancient chants, prophesies, poetry, and prognostications. I have also learned that two other dialects come through at times, Canamari and Tucano."

We could tell from the way Janet spoke and her poise onstage that she was an educated and intelligent woman. "My tapes have been played for the Yanomami people, and they have danced around the recorder and rejoiced at the spoken words. The latest tapes of the Canamari language have been a breakthrough as well, for it shows the languages continue to emerge, offering new messages for different tribes."

Then she spoke the languages for us, without going into a trance, with as much fluency, emotion, and conviction as anyone fluent in any language. Even though she still had no clue what she was saying, nor did we, at one point she laughed, as if she were telling a joke. Then she chanted, and toward the end, her voice became somber, and she began to cry. The entire audience appeared moved.

During her presentation, someone tugged on the back of my chair. I turned to see if Jim had bumped me. Both his hands rested on the table and were nowhere near me. No one sat on the other side of me, and I looked down the aisle to see if someone had just passed me. Everyone was seated, enthralled by Janet's story. Perhaps someone behind me had kicked my chair. But as I turned around, I could see that the tables were placed far enough away from each other that unless the woman at the other table had scooted herself down and tapped my chair leg with her toe, she couldn't have reached it. Besides, it didn't feel like a tap. It was a tug.

The next day, psychologist Jeffery Tarrant, PhD, hooked Janet up to an electroencephalograph so we could witness her brain waves while at rest and not speaking, while she spoke English, and when she spoke the unwritten tribal languages. He and Janet had been working together for about fourteen months, he said.

He first explained in simple terms the different brain waves. Delta waves are when you're in a deep sleep or unconscious. Theta waves are when you're in a twilight state (nodding off), daydreaming, or in a creative state. Alpha waves are when you're in a resting state, neutral, relaxed attention. And beta waves are for cortical processing (wakefulness). He said that theta and alpha waves are dominant during meditation, that novices meditate in alpha. The longer you meditate, the deeper it goes into theta.

During the presentation, we all watched in silent fascination. He'd switch from showing us the brain waves to colored imaging of which parts of the brain were being used. When Janet was at rest, not much brain wave activity showed and little color on the image. When she spoke English, her frontal lobe lit up in red. When she spoke the tribal languages, not only did her frontal lobe light up, but also her right temporal and occipital lobes. Dr. Tarrant switched to the brain wave graph, and all of her brain waves were all over the place.

He said that the area of her brain activated the most was the area science has identified as the one for forgiveness, where you have to put yourself aside.

At the buffet-style lunch with cold cuts, cheeses, breads, and various salads, Lisa and Tom Butler, the two presenters on electronic voice phenomena (or EVPs), happened to sit by us. A couple about our age, Lisa was more outgoing than Tom and started conversing immediately. Both were Spiritualists from Reno, Nevada; they belonged to the Spiritualist High Desert Church of Reno, but they recently voted to change the name to the Spiritualist Society of Reno to attract more members. Both had taken the courses through the Morris Pratt Institute and were ordained Spiritualist ministers.

We told them we had just visited the two Spiritualist churches in Vegas, and they were familiar with both. I mentioned the reading I'd received from Rev. Virginia and her bringing up Jim's ex-wife's name, and they said that Rev. Virginia was really good.

They gave their presentation on the second day of the conference. Before they began, I wondered how they would fill a two-hour presentation on EVPs and how they captured spirit voices on tape, but their presentation was quite interesting and compelling. EVP is the "term traditionally used to describe anomalous, intelligible speech recorded in or produced by electronic devices, and for which no currently understood physical explanations can account." She said the way you can tell it's an EVP is that the voice won't sound quite human. "EVP have a distinctive character of cadence, pitch, frequency, volume, and use of background sound. The voices have a distinctive sound to them that is difficult to describe. For instance, EVP messages often have an unusual speed of enunciation; the words seem to be spoken more quickly than normal human speech."

Along with giving the background of how she and Tom became involved in this area, Lisa added that "there's a new generation of therapists who suggest that patients who maintain a bond with the deceased are better adjusted through the grief process." She said, "Ask your loved ones to talk to you. They're people, too. They want you to ask questions."

She told one story about a woman who was busy getting ready for the holidays. She had let her dog in and was wrapping presents. A friend came by and invited her to go shopping. Not one to turn down a shopping trip, the woman left everything as it was with the dog inside. When she returned home, she found the gifts she had been wrapping in shambles. This woman kept a voice-activated digital recorder, and when she played back the recorder, she heard her daughter's voice call out the dog's name and say, "No!" Her daughter had passed away a number of years prior.

In between some of the lecture sessions, the certified mediums demonstrated. Although Jim and I didn't receive any messages from our loved ones, with one demonstrating right after another, it became clear to both of us that there was a big difference in mediumship training and delivery style. Clearly, Kim Russo was the more experienced and polished medium. One woman, who looked in her forties with bleached blond hair and heavy makeup, was rather overbearing, bullying the recipients, "Yes or no!" after she gave a piece of evidence. She didn't even give the person a chance to think about whether the information was correct. When the recipient said no, which was quite often, her condescending response was, "Well, that's what I'm getting. I have to trust what spirit's giving me." Then she'd go back to pacing up and down the aisle, swaying her hips as if she were a runway model. It was obvious her ego got in the way of her mediumship. We hoped we wouldn't get a reading from her.

Another woman had a gentler, kinder manner about her. Also looking in her forties with long, naturally blond hair, she worked as a high school teacher in her day job. She moved among the audience as well, but she didn't strut her stuff like the other medium had. At one point, she walked up to me and asked if I'd lost a child. I said I hadn't. It turned out she was with the lady in front of me.

Janet of the tribal tongues also demonstrated her mediumship, and I liked her method the best. She brought humor to her readings. It was nice to see that those in the spirit world kept their sense of humor.

Bully medium aside, the rest connected with deceased loved ones easily, as if it were the most natural thing in the world to do.

We later visited with Lisa and Tom again at their booth, where we bought their book on collecting EVPs, *There Is No Death, There Are No Dead*. I told Lisa my goal to become a medium, and she recommended the Morris Pratt courses.

She reached forward from behind the booth and grabbed both of my hands that had been resting on the table. "Do the whole thing," she said, "not just the mediumship coursework. Get involved in healing. That's one of the fastest ways to open the lines of communication."

Once home, and after I had processed everything I'd learned at the afterlife conference, something remarkable stood out to me. Not once did anyone mention God, Jesus, or any religion during the whole conference. Not a single message from spirit communication, either at the conference or at the Spiritualist churches, urged the living to go to church, or to accept Jesus as our lord and savior, or to turn our lives over to God. Not a single message delivered by any of the mediums said, "He says he's with God," or "She says she's in heaven with Jesus." I found it ironic that we spent an entire weekend at a conference devoted to the afterlife and attended two Spiritualist churches, yet no medium mentioned these things when they gave readings and evidence for the afterlife. It seemed to me that the afterlife maybe *is* more about a quantum consciousness than anything mystical or religious. As Loyd Auerbach said in one of his presentations, "Medium communication gives us a consensus of the afterlife that we've never gotten from religions."

Jim had often said in our discussions about our journey, although he wasn't trying to become a medium, that the foundation of all religions was the same: it's supposed to be about love and compassion, but (male) church leaders need to impose rules, guilt, and fear in its members and exclude anyone who isn't like-minded. Nearly every religion believes it is the one true religion. They can't all be the one true religion. Even materialistic science has become a religion of sorts, using fear, ridicule, and exclusion if, heaven forbid, someone should venture into "pseudoscience" and accept the evidence for psychic ability and consciousness survival.

Jessica Maxwell made this point in her spiritual memoir, *Roll Around Heaven*, which applied not only to religion but to mainstream science as well: "Any version of a spiritual tradition that preaches discrimination against other groups, insists that its way is the only way, and/or offers fear and guilt to its people instead of love, forgiveness, and reverence—well, sorry but these guys just don't get it."

Kim Russo said, too, that our lives in the physical world and the afterlife come down to love, unity, and peace. We always have options, no matter which side of the veil we're on or on which side of the science debate we're on. We can choose to be loving, compassionate, and kind, or we can choose not to be. It doesn't get simpler than that.

We all, at one time or another, question the meaning of life, why we're here, what our purpose is for walking this earth. I left the afterlife conference convinced that pantheism still resonated with me, that humankind should have reverence and awe for everything because everything in the Universe is connected. As for a religion and way of life, Spiritualism, to me, with its lack of human-imposed rules, guilt, and fear-based dogma, and its acceptance of tolerance, diversity, free will, love, and universal harmony also comes closest to my truth. Pantheism and Spiritualism seemed like they would make a happy couple.

CHAPTER 16

Feeling Spirit

It happened in Olive Garden of all places, nearing a year into my journey. We were having dinner with genealogy friends, Dorothy and John, a couple older than we were. They came to Salt Lake to do research at the Family History Library. We had known them for years but hadn't seen them in more than a decade.

As the waiter set down our meals, the heavenly aroma of garlic wafting in my nostrils, Dorothy talked about the times when John would pick up her dad and drive him to their house for a visit, two hundred miles away in one direction. During these four-hour drives, her dad told John stories about his life that he'd never shared with her. We all lamented that John hadn't had a recorder with him. As she shared this tale in between bites of her meal, I experienced an intense, sharp pain on the right side of my head. Only someone who's studying to be a medium would think that the pain might not be hers. Normal people would think it was their own pain and rush to the emergency room for an MRI.

I winced, set my fork down, and put my hand to my head. I wanted to ask Dorothy, "Did your father die of something in the head, a blow to the head or an aneurysm?" But I figured that would raise too many eyebrows. When she paused in the story, I asked instead, "What did your dad die from?" Later, Jim told me that my question came so out of context for the conversation that he wondered where it came from.

It must have taken Dorothy by surprise, too, because it seemed to take her a second or two to transition her thoughts from the story she told to her dad's death.

She's going to say he died from a heart attack, I thought, *or kidney failure or pneumonia or something.* When she responded, I nearly fell out of my chair.

"It was a brain tumor."

She might as well have punched me in the solar plexus, so stunned was I. Then the pain in my head dissipated, as if a tumor had burst.

It happened! My first validated spirit communication. But it also created my first ethical dilemma as a budding medium. I pushed risotto around my plate with my fork. My pulse quickened as I wrestled with myself whether to tell Dorothy and John, both devout Catholics, what I'd just experienced. As they continued reminiscing, her dad then made me feel happy that he was remembered, and they continued to talk about him.

Crap. He's with us. Now what do I do?

I didn't know all the ethics of mediumship, but I knew enough to know that you shouldn't approach someone who hadn't asked for a reading. Theresa Captuo, of *Long Island Medium*, however, did it all the time on her show. Having done some television in my career as a genealogist, I knew these were all staged, and each person had to sign a waiver for their image to appear on television.

Dorothy and John certainly hadn't asked for a reading. I didn't even know what their beliefs were about the afterlife or spirit communication. That's not something that typically comes up in everyday conversation. They didn't know that I was developing my mediumistic abilities, and if they asked for more, could I deliver right there in Olive Garden over my grilled chicken Toscano and parmesan risotto?

But what was my obligation to spirit? I had asked for this ability. Her dad didn't come through just to validate for me that I could communicate with him. He came for them.

In the end, I decided not to say anything.

On the car ride home, as I told Jim what had happened, I still had a mild, overall headache. I didn't know whether or not this was residual energy or if Dorothy's dad hadn't left me. Just in case, I communicated telepathically, "You have to stay with Dorothy, not with me. I'm sorry I couldn't say anything, but if I'm meant to deliver a message, you and the Universe will have to arrange another time when I'll know that she'll be open to receiving it."

I felt bad. After all this, had I let down the spirit world?

I read Janet Nohavec's book *Where Two Worlds Meet: How to Develop Evidential Mediumship*. She, too, is certified by the Forever Family Foundation, as well as by a Spiritualist church. A Catholic nun who left the convent to practice mediumship, she eventually became a Spiritualist minister. In her book, she says, "Remember this: The spirit people never waste a thought. . . . There's a reason you get what you get. Always."

The problem remained: I had no sitters. I didn't have anyone on whom to practice. By this time, I had read as many mediumship guidebooks as I could, but I'd yet to find a development circle, a class, or someone to mentor me. My year timeline was also running out. I had a couple of weeks left. While so much had happened to convince me that my psychic faculties were opening, and spirit gave me physical evidence from flowers falling down to a pain in my head, I sure didn't consider myself a medium.

I looked into the Morris Pratt courses again, but I needed practical experience, not more book learning. Then I remembered Lisa Butler's words from the afterlife conference: "Get involved in healing. That's one of the fastest ways to open the lines of communication."

Okay. I'd still be on the same path, just taking a different direction. I was too invested to give up now. A second year was needed.

CHAPTER 17

Different Path,
Same Destination

Lisa neglected to tell me what kind of healing I should learn, and much later I would realize she meant spiritual healing or healing mediumship. That kind of healing, according to the great spiritual healer Harry Edwards (1893–1976), meant that the medium works with specific healing guides and helpers, often doctors and health care providers in the spirit world; the spirit world does the healing, working on behalf of God, and the healing medium must attune to these guides and issue the healing directive.

But I was ignorant of all this then, and as it's said, everything happens for a reason. Instead, I came across a healing method called Reiki (pronounced RAY-kee) when I searched online. It resonated with my worldview about pantheism, the Universe, and spirit. The word *Reiki* comes from the Japanese word *Rei*, which means universal life force, and *Ki*, which means energy. According to Kathie Lipinski, RN, MSN, and Reiki master teacher, in her article, "Making Reiki Real,"

> Reiki is spiritually guided life force energy. This means that it
> has a higher intelligence, knows what the person needs, and

is guided by the Higher power or Higher self of the person. A person receiving a Reiki treatment gets what they need at the time. It brings the highest healing for all concerned . . .

Reiki is a balancing energy. What is in excess, Reiki lessens (like pain). What is lacking, Reiki increases and fills. So one can say that Reiki restores and balances one's physical, mental, and emotional energies. It puts one's physical body in the best condition to promote healing. When people are anxious, Reiki relaxes them. When they are in pain, Reiki can reduce or eliminate it. When people are emotionally upset, Reiki can calm them and balance their emotions so that they can see their situation and problems more clearly.

On Amazon, I discovered hundreds of books about Reiki, and settled on *Reiki for Life: The Complete Guide to Reiki Practice for Levels 1, 2, & 3* by Penelope Quest. This is where I discovered that there are at least three levels of Reiki "attunement," the process of becoming initiated or "attuned" to Reiki energy and becoming a channel for Reiki. You receive these attunements from a Reiki master teacher, and this is the reason healing and channeling abilities can be developed so quickly. Spiritual empowerment is passed from master teacher to student. "Being attuned to Reiki," says Quest, "can often unblock [psychic] ability or allow you to develop it further than you would have otherwise done." Ah-ha! This was exactly what I needed. Now to find a Reiki class. That proved easier than finding mediumship classes.

On the Google search page, the fourth listing showed a woman named Carla, a Reiki master teacher. Feeling drawn to her webpage, I looked at no others. I read her bio and credentials, which included a doctorate and a postdoctoral fellowship in clinical psychology, and she held membership in the American Association of Integrative Medicine. She'd taught more than thirty different health and psychology courses for several universities, and her Reiki courses were approved for continuing education credits. I didn't need the credits, but this added legitimacy to her courses. When I opened her CV and it was longer than mine, I thought, *She's the one.*

I sent her an email and explained my goal of wanting to learn Reiki but also to become a medium. She responded quickly, and wrote, "Mrs. Takata only taught channeling to three of her twenty-two masters and one of them is in my lineage, which includes channeling in second degree and also involves an extra third eye attunement to increase those clairvoyant abilities; all of my students who complete second degree are able to do mediumship work, although some are called to do it more than others so if you are interested in developing this ability, you contacted the right person."

Mrs. Who? The only lineage I knew about was by blood. But *all* of her students can do mediumship work? That's an amazing claim. I had my doubts. If anyone would be the exception to the rule, it would be me. In my house, we have what's known as the "Sharon Test." Something Jim thinks he's fixed can be working perfectly, but when I test it, it won't work. Might as well put the old Sharon Test to work on the Reiki classes. The first degree Reiki class (Reiki I) was held all day on one Saturday, then the second degree (Reiki II) was all day on the following Saturday. I signed up.

"Maybe I'll stay in a motel for the next four days," Jim said during our morning tea, after I read to him the prep for my Reiki class attunements that Carla had emailed.

For four to seven days prior, I was to eliminate alcohol (no glass of wine with dinner), eliminate or cut back on smoking (not a problem; I don't smoke), eliminate or minimize consuming sugar products, including *chocolate* (torture, I tell you), eliminate or reduce consumption of caffeine (I drink three cups of tea a day), eliminate or minimize all meats (they carry negative energy from their slaughter), and if possible, go on a physician-approved fast for one to three days or an all-fruit-and-vegetable diet.

I began a week before the class to wean myself off caffeine so I wouldn't get a headache. I was down to just one cup in the morning, and so far, the reduction in caffeine hadn't bothered me—until Figaro came into the kitchen looking for food after he'd already been fed. "Do you want some milk?" He often drank a little milk when he saw me get the carton out for my cereal. As I poured about a tablespoon into a custard cup, I mentioned to Jim how much calmer I felt now that I tried to live by the five Reiki principles Carla had sent. I must have recited them at least 589 times a day. It's amazing what a little self-brainwashing can do.

1. Just for today, do not anger.
2. Just for today, do not worry.
3. Honor parents, teachers, and elders.
4. Earn an honest living.
5. Have gratitude for all living beings.

As I turned to set the milk down, Figaro trotted out of the kitchen and headed toward the sliding glass door in the dining room to be let outside. "Get back here, you little shit!"

"I don't think you should cut out that last cup of tea," Jim said.

I eliminated wine, sugar, and chocolate, stuck with only one cup of caffeinated tea first thing in the morning, said goodbye to all meat—asking Jim, "There's no trauma involved in laying eggs or giving milk for cheese, is there?"—and ate normally otherwise.

I awoke at five, even though class didn't begin until nine, too excited to sleep any later. I arrived at Carla's apartment promptly and could hear voices chatting. Carla answered the door, looking about ten or so years older than her photograph on her website. I couldn't fault her there. The photo on my website showed me a good ten or so pounds ago.

She still had long, highlighted, dishwater-blond hair parted down the middle, and wore a purple top, black leggings, and flip-flops. She greeted me with a hug, then introduced me to the two ladies already seated in her living room, Lina and Terry. Both smiled and looked in their forties.

Carla's living room was small with a black leather couch and two wicker chairs. The sage aroma when I entered permeated my nostrils and lingered in my lungs as if I'd walked into a house that had recently been gutted by a fire. I didn't think I'd ever stop exhaling it. Against one wall stood a waist-high Asian cabinet, on top of which sat five brass Buddhas. Even though the first day of spring came two days prior, it was still chilly, so Carla's gas fireplace was lit. On the fireplace mantel sat a Buddha head and unframed photographs of Dr. Mikao Usui, Dr. Chujiro Hayahi, and Mrs. Hawayo Takata. *Ah. So that's who Mrs. Takata is.* Carla later explained her "lineage"—that is, who taught whom. A water fountain on a kitchen bar trickled.

Carla sat in a wicker chair with her back to the fireplace, while Lina, Terry, and I occupied the couch and chair opposite her.

With immense energy and humor, Carla gave a little of her background and mentioned living in Las Vegas.

"Did you grow up in Vegas?" I asked.

"No. I lived there a couple of years when I was in high school."

I didn't want to deviate from her lesson, but I had to ask which high school. Don't ask me how, but I already knew what she was going to say.

"I went to Valley," she said.

"When was that?" Given that she had three grown children, I suspected she was older than I, probably in her early sixties.

"1968."

"I graduated from Valley in 1974."

The other ladies looked stunned, as did Carla. She repeated, "Valley High School?"

"Yep. Valley High School."

"Wow. We'll have to talk about that later."

Carla had us share about ourselves and what brought us to Reiki. I gave the *Reader's Digest* version, recapping the last year of my journey to become a medium and feeling like I kept getting blocked. "Last November," I told them, "I attended a conference on the afterlife sponsored by the Forever Family Foundation. I told a Spiritualist minister about my blocks, and she said the quickest way to mediumship is through healing work."

Lina, chubby and with short, curly, light-brown hair, wore glasses. She sat next to me on the sofa and said she was a victim of childhood abuse, but she wanted to take Reiki to help her daughter. She called her an "HSP," a "highly sensitive person." I'd never heard of this type of person. Lina's daughter was twenty-one and had been through all sorts of treatments that hadn't helped. Lina described herself as an empath, a person affected by other people's energies.

Terry, a brunette with shoulder-length hair, said she was raised by a dad who believed in Native American spirit guides and a mom who was a Church of Christ member. She said she still had skepticism about a supernatural force, but she was trying to reconcile what her father taught her and what her mother believed about "dabbling in the occult." She came because someone suggested Reiki might help her daughter, who has TMJ, temporomandibular joints.

Hmm. I wondered if Reiki would heal my daughter's skepticism.

All three of us had Googled Reiki classes in Salt Lake City and found Carla. Even though there were other Reiki teachers in the area, Carla's credentials had impressed us. But I was clueless about what to expect from the classes and how much ritual was involved. Rituals reminded me of the Catholic Church.

Carla gave each of us a one-inch binder with handouts for the class. We reviewed the pages that explained what Reiki is and isn't, saying that you don't "give" Reiki but that the recipient is like a sponge who soaks up the energy they need. It comes *through* us, as if we were a hollow reed, not *from* us. Reiki comes from the Universal Source. After attunement, you "intend" for Reiki to flow by saying a short, opening prayer of intention. Then, whenever you place your hands on someone or something (a plant or animal), Reiki energy begins flowing. "Hands on, Reiki on. Hands off, Reiki off," Carla said.

I knew Reiki would be difficult to explain to someone unfamiliar with the practice, especially to Laurie. She would now have to deal with her mother taking a detour. So, I asked Carla for her "elevator speech." She said, "It's a hands-on healing modality." Seriously? I wasn't even sure what a "modality" was, so how would other people know what that is? I guess my elevator speech will be "a hands-on healing method"; then if someone wants to know more, they'll ask. She said it's unethical to send distant Reiki healing to someone who hasn't asked for the healing. Hmmm. That was curious. People pray for other people without asking their permission. Why would sending healing to someone be unethical? I didn't have time to ask, though. Carla had moved on.

She had us set aside our binders and led us through a guided meditation while she prepared the room for our attunements. She told us she'd be smudging the room (again?) with white sage—I still hadn't gotten the scent out of my nostrils from her pre-class smudging—but she didn't elaborate any further. She had us close our eyes, and, while still seated, we were to place our left hand over our belly button area, then our right hand on top of the left.

"Imagine your breath is filling a bottle and raising your hands on your body," she said. "Do this ten times."

I heard her by the fireplace, then smelled the pungent smoke of sage. As she came near me with sage, it was difficult to continue taking deep breaths and not cough. Sage fumes reminded me of the peat fires that Jim and I smelled in tourist cottages in Ireland. It was suffocating. I didn't know how our Irish ancestors tolerated it. They must have been a sickly lot with lung issues.

"Now envision yourself at the beach," Carla said. (Here we go again with a beach. Why can't we lounge poolside and sip mai tais garnished with little umbrellas?) "Feel the warm sand between your toes. Ground yourself in the sand." She led us as we imagined the spray of the ocean and wind on our faces, then we looked at the sunshine. "Feel engulfed by the light and radiate the light."

I could hear her moving around the living room and was tempted to peek, but figured I'd blow any chances of being empowered with Reiki if I did. I didn't want to get kicked out of the class for cheating.

Then she brought us back to the "physical world." I was so consumed by the sage that I was pretty sure I hadn't left it.

When I opened my eyes, I saw that she had brought one of the dining room chairs into the living room. She had Lina sit in the wicker chair where Carla had been sitting, and she directed me to the dining room chair, which had its back to Lina and Terry. It was time for our attunements to the Reiki energy. She instructed us to close our eyes and place our hands in *gassho* position, palms together and placed in front of the heart.

I heard Carla move behind Terry first, then she went to Lina, and finally me. From behind me, she placed her hands on my shoulders rather firmly, then she tapped my right shoulder once. From behind me still, she reached around me, took my hands and raised them above my head, opened them, blew on them, then put them back. She did this about six times, blowing a puff of air (Reiki) on my open palms, then placing my opened hands on various places of my body—my head, at my throat, and my heart. She opened and tapped them, then closed them. Then she whispered in my ear, something about going forth in light and love.

After our attunements, we all sat on the floor cross-legged, with Carla in the front, me behind her, Terry behind me, then Lina. Carla directed us to put our hands on the shoulders of the person in front. She asked me if I felt anything in my hands, and I said I didn't. (The Sharon Test never fails.) I was still skeptical about how one person could "attune" another person. It seemed like magical, woo-woo thinking. But Carla said she felt the heat from my palms on her shoulders, particularly on the left shoulder. She asked what I felt, and I said the heat from Terry's hands.

"Is one warmer than the other?" she asked.

When I focused my attention on Terry's hands, I, too, thought there was more heat on the left side. Terry and Lina both agreed that it was the left side for both of them, too.

Then Carla stood up and announced it was time for lunch. What? No gong?

When we reconvened an hour later, Carla had us turn to a page in our binders and explained the Usui Reiki symbols. She taught us the first one, called the power symbol, the one she attuned us to. We should draw this symbol on our hands with a finger or over someone in the air before we did any healing. As I practiced, it reminded me of a priest making the sign of the cross over the congregation.

Carla had us do a ten-minute self-healing. We went through the hand positions again, and this time, I wrote down the order: eyes, temples, ears, back of head, then upper chest, heart, solar plexus, and abdomen. She put on New Age music, which, for me, sounded a little loud. I've always had sensitive hearing and don't like loud anything.

She said to do our prayer before any healing, putting our hands together in gassho position, thanking our lineage masters, then inviting the Universe, our guides, guardian angles, master teachers, to guide us as a channel for Reiki. She included in her prayer Jesus, Buddha, and the Virgin Mary, so I figured it couldn't hurt to invite them all to join Team Sharon, too, as well as all the saints. Now I had more players than an Australian football team. I'm not sure why Joseph never gets included. I guess when he missed that child support payment, he became a deadbeat dad.

I zipped through the healing, mostly because I didn't have any sense of time, and didn't want to be the only one still on the first healing position when she called time. Since we had just returned from lunch, I also hadn't quieted my mind. I was still in "I don't want to be late" mode and belching the veggie sandwich I'd eaten.

After I finished, I put my hands in gassho position again, then time seemed to drag. Since I hadn't experienced anything in my hands when we played train before lunch, I put my hands open and facing up on my lap, which was how I normally meditated. I waited until I felt the energy there, then did the self-healing positions again. My palms felt warm and a little tingly now. I moved a little slower, but apparently, a little too fast. When I returned my hands to gassho again, I sat for several minutes before I heard Lina whispering to Terry. When Carla heard us talking, she came out of her bedroom. I know it had to have been longer than ten minutes.

We talked about the twenty-one-day cleansing period. This is when you experience a vibrational shift, Carla told us, as your body rids itself of toxins, and the chakras each cycle three times, hence the twenty-one days.

"You don't have to do anything during this period," Carla said. "Just be aware of your body ridding itself of toxins. After Reiki I, the cleansing is more physical, so you may experience achiness, dizziness, coughing, constipation, diarrhea, and frequent urination."

I typically pee a lot anyway because I sip tea throughout the day, but I had already noticed the need to pee a lot more since the attunement. I hadn't had that much liquid.

"After Reiki II next week," she continued, "the cleanse is more emotional. You might find yourself getting angry, frustrated, fearful, or experiencing grief, sadness, or crying for no apparent reason." *Great. I guess Jim had better stay in a motel.*

Now we would enter the sacred space and practice healings on each other. Carla used her other bedroom as her Reiki room. In the center was a Reiki (or massage) table. Against one wall stood another waist-high Asian dresser with her crystal healing bowls. Across the room sat a desk, and on it, a crystal grid with a large amethyst in the center, a rose quartz, and several clear quartz crystals positioned around the amethyst.

Lina climbed on the table and lay on her back while Carla demonstrated the hand positions, then had Terry and me do them. Terry and I switched places with Lina so she could practice the hand positions.

"Okay," said Carla, "You'll work in teams, with one on the table, one working on the head, and the other on the torso. I'll leave you for ten minutes, then I'll come back in and tell you when the person on the table needs to turn over." She left us.

Terry volunteered to receive Reiki first. I did the head positions, and Lina did her torso, and then we both worked on Terry's legs and feet. We clearly didn't have any sense of time; we finished about a minute or so before Carla came back to tell us that Terry should roll onto her stomach.

While Lina and I placed our hands on Terry's back, I heard a smoke alarm going off over the music Carla left on. I was tempted to shut the music off so I could determine where the noise came from. But I figured that would interrupt everything. Then it occurred to me that the smoke alarm I heard had something to do with Terry. My hands burned. I got hot all over and even began sweating.

After the session, Carla asked Terry to sit up and tell us what she experienced. She said she'd had a headache, and that the coolness of my hands on her forehead felt good. That surprised me, as I thought my hands were hot and that her forehead felt warm. I even wondered if she had a fever.

Carla then asked me about my experience. I looked at Terry and said, "This is going to sound really weird, but were you or someone you know in a fire? I kept hearing a smoke detector going off when I had my hands on your back heart chakra."

She thought a minute, and said, "No." I felt disappointed, but then she smiled with a gleam in her eyes. "But . . ."

It turned out that she sometimes feels like she's being watched by a spirit, and there's fire around this person; plus, she recently had a dream about a friend who was around a lot of heat (it turned out he was camping and around a campfire); plus, she *loves* fire!

Carla said, "You mean starting fires?"

Great, I thought, *I'm in class with a pyromaniac.*

Terry said she has always had a fascination with fire, and when she was a kid, she loved building the campfires, and she still loves being around fire, like fireplaces.

"So, you do have a strong connection with fire?" I said.

"Yes."

My shock turned into a high. This was the first time I'd read a complete stranger psychically.

When my turn came to get on the table, I felt chilled the whole time my classmates did healing on me, probably because I'd been so hot and sweaty while practicing Reiki on Terry. Lina definitely put too much pressure on my head. She gave me a headache. Terry's hands felt on fire, and I faintly heard the smoke alarm again.

After my session, I told Carla about the chills, but I honestly didn't feel anything else. Lina said she felt an energy pull when she placed her hands on the back of my head. Perhaps she pulled out the headache she'd given when she put her hands on my forehead. Terry said my back felt really hot where she had her hands, but I thought it was the fire energy she carries. Carla didn't comment on any of it, which disappointed me.

After our practice session, Carla talked about the "clairs" (clairvoyance, clairaudience, etc.), and she said we should take note of our strengths in these areas. I said I was more clairaudient, only because I had heard the smoke alarm, but I also saw images on occasion in my mind's eye. She said when we get our third-eye attunement next week, it would enhance our psychic and mediumship abilities. I still had my doubts that it would be that simple for someone else to attune me and I'd magically become a medium. None of the mediumship guidebooks mentioned this. But I had paid for the two classes, so why not?

CHAPTER 18

What Was Happening
to Me?

Everyone has aspects about themselves they wish they could change, or areas in their life that bring discontent. I'm a well-ordered person who likes routine, and when something happens to disrupt it, I don't make lemonade from the lemons; I prefer to pucker and wallow in the distaste of it all. After more than a year of nightly meditation, however, disruptions no longer affected me as they had before—like when my computer hard drive crashed and the technician said, "Are you backed up?" or when internet service went out on the day I needed to be online in my classes. I remained calm and dealt with the problems without panic or drama.

I noticed other changes in myself that occurred without me trying to consciously change. I no longer obsessed as I had about growing old, my weight, or my cholesterol. I slept more soundly. Before bed, I used an abbreviated meditation that I called my "gratitude meditation." I took seven deep, cleansing breaths, one for each of the seven energy centers. When I returned my breathing to normal, I asked the spirit world to surround Jim and me in white light, letting only positive energy in. Then I thanked the Universe, Team Sharon, and all the spirit people for their guidance, for the wonderful day I had, for the awesome journey my soul has chosen, that I have a healthy body, and for all the people and things in my life I'm grateful for. Often, before I finished, I had drifted into a deep slumber.

No longer did I have panic attacks in the evenings, when I would second-guess something I'd said or done during the day or fret about something in the future. If my thoughts turned to those things, I gave myself permission to worry about them tomorrow. By then, I'd engaged in my daily routine and was too busy to occupy my mind with those thoughts. When I woke in the night to pee, I went back to sleep quickly by telling myself, "You're asleep now," and I focused on my breathing.

Although I'd considered myself a compassionate person, I always had significantly more compassion for animals (cats in particular) than people. If someone expressed an unfortunate situation in their life, I never, ever said, "I'll pray for you," or "I'll keep you in my prayers," mostly because I didn't believe in God, and I didn't pray. I would say instead that I'd keep the person in my thoughts, or "I'll send good thoughts out to the Universe for you," and that was the end of that.

Now I started setting aside time each morning for a five-minute "heart meditation." I focused my breathing on my heart and asked the Universe to help me have more compassion for others and to help me have unconditional love, reverence, and awe for all beings. Then I actually did send love, healing, and positive thoughts out for those I said I would. I asked the Universe to help my family and friends to find their own path and peace, whatever that meant for their souls' journeys. I sent love and healing to family and friends who had crossed over. I sent apologies to those I'd hurt, especially to my mother, and forgave those who had hurt me. After a few weeks of this "heart meditation," I felt lighter. I no longer held any grudges against anyone, including myself. I knew I had hurt people in my life (who hasn't?), but in forgiving myself for those acts of unkindness, I also accepted them as part of my soul's journey from which I was to learn a lesson: to be more kind, compassionate, and forgiving.

Does prayer actually work? Some studies say no, others yes. Does this morning meditation make me feel more grounded, calm, and at peace throughout the day? If the prayers and healing I sent for others actually work in reverse for my spiritual growth, then, yes, it worked.

Then there was the biggie. For much of my life, I've worried about money. At one point, my ex-husband and I were in quite a bit of debt, which gave me nightly insomnia and daily anxiety. Then I was serendipitously offered a position as an acquisitions editor for a publishing company—a job I hadn't even sought or known was available. At about the same time, a client with deep pockets hired me for a long-term project. Again, it just fell into my lap. That client sent me and Dwight to Ireland twice and provided a steady part-time income for the next thirteen years. Overnight, it seemed, I made enough to get us out of debt. For once, we had a savings, and I paid for Laurie's bachelor's degree out of pocket. These events were long before I started on this journey, but now I could see how spirit tried to get my attention. Either I was incredibly lucky, or the spirit world manifested opportunities for me.

As a self-employed person, my income has always fluctuated, and even though I've kept myself out of debt since then, I've continued to worry about money. After I started meditating, one day it dawned on me that I wasn't thinking about money as much as I had been. I trusted that I would always have enough money to live comfortably and for the things I desire. Fortunately, I don't have grandiose desires and live a financially simple life. I mostly desire more books.

Meditation has changed my life in so many ways, but by also accepting the scientific evidence that consciousness survives physical death, it liberated me. Life was not too short. I didn't need to have a "bucket list," well, except to get rid of stuff so Laurie wouldn't be stuck with it all. I didn't have to accomplish all of my goals while I resided on the physical plane. I wouldn't have to be constantly on the go and plan every piece of my future. I could relax and enjoy today. Time is an illusion for those of us here in the physical world; in the afterlife, there is no time. When I shed my physical body, I will continue to exist in another form. Places I want to go, things I want to do, people I want to see will be a thought away. Eternity is now.

I no longer feared dying or the death of my loved ones. They will still be with me, and I will be with them when I cross over. I will still be with Laurie and watch over her kids and see her grandkids grow old. It still bothers me, though, that she won't be looking for signs I send her. Of course, if Jim dies before me, I will miss him terribly. But I know he will be with me in spirit, guiding me and looking out for me until we are reunited in the spirit world.

All this new personal growth was an unexpected and wonderful benefit of my journey. But I still wasn't having a two-way conversation with dead people.

CHAPTER 19

Another Path, Same Destination

I would love to tell you that the second half of Reiki, the attunement to open my third eye, magically made me a medium. But it didn't. Nor did the third level of Reiki or becoming a Reiki master. I would love to tell you that I experienced all, or even some, of the emotions Carla said would be part of the cleansing. I didn't. I either had an impenetrable soul, or I didn't require an emotional purging. The most positive part of my Reiki studies was my mediation practice. Carla was a huge proponent of meditation, and I found myself meditating for longer periods—up to thirty minutes on some days. Meditation continued to benefit me in my daily life in ways I hadn't expected. I was also unquestionably more psychic, more in tune with myself and others, but the dead weren't talking. Or if they were, I was still deaf to them.

At the afterlife conference, a woman I had sat with at one lunch said she knew someone in Park City, Utah, a shaman and medium, who might be able to mentor me. Then, at home, in *Prevention* magazine, an article on shamanism drew my eye. I took this as a sign. While my search for the person in Park City was a bust, I found someone closer in the Salt Lake City area. Dr. Michael Walker was not only a shamanic practitioner and teacher but also a medical doctor, held a PhD in neuroscience, and was a professor at a university medical school. He had served on the board of directors for the Society of Shamanic Practitioners and had trained in a three-year program through the Foundation for Shamanic Studies with Sandra Ingerman, a renowned shamanic practitioner. The best part was he took students on a one-to-one mentoring basis.

Surely Dr. Walker's credentials would impress Laurie as much as they had me, and she would realize that respected scientists didn't see all this as woo-woo and pseudoscience. I knew, though, that if I continued to push her, I could drive her further away. She had already told me we would *never* agree on this. But surely this would cause her to rethink her position, and of course, I couldn't wait to tell her. When I did, it made no difference. I received the same cool, indifferent response. She just wasn't interested. The door kept slamming in my face like I was some kind of Jehovah's Witness missionary for the spirit world. Or worse. Like someone selling carpet cleaning services. Why couldn't I keep my damn mouth shut?

When I spoke with Dr. Walker over the phone, one of the first things he told me was I won't become a "shaman." That's an earned, honorary title bestowed upon someone by a community. He called himself not a shaman but a shamanic practitioner and teacher. He said he teaches Core Shamanism—the term was foreign to me—as taught by Sandra Ingerman and also Michael Harner. He would teach me how to journey, how to work with spirits, and how to do a soul retrieval. Working with spirits caught my ear, and I told him my goal was to be a medium.

When I arrived at Dr. Walker's house, a man of average height with short, white, silky hair and a white stubble on his face stood out front. He wasn't wearing beads and feathers as I had imagined a shamanic practitioner would. Just a simple short-sleeved, button-down shirt and slacks. After we said hello and introduced ourselves, he said, "I'm just watching this rattlesnake in my yard."

I followed his gaze to the rattlesnake right there in the middle of his front yard. I asked if he often had them. He said, "No. This is the first one I've seen in the five years we've lived here."

I said, "It must be a sign." I didn't know of what, but I knew that the snake was there for a reason at that particular moment in time. He grinned but didn't offer any interpretation; then he led me into his home.

We sat in his dimly lit basement family room, he on a worn love seat on one side of the room, and me opposite him on the matching couch. The room smelled of sage, although thankfully not as overpowering as it had been in my Reiki classes. A candle burned on the stand that also held a TV. Hanging on the walls were drums and paintings of bears and other wild animals. A small bookcase contained books on shamanism, and there were also a number of crystals placed around the room. Then a cat appeared, and I knew I must be in the right place. I'm not shy about being a cat lady.

We made small talk, his voice soft and soothing. I restated my goals of becoming a medium, and how I was told that the quickest way is through healing. I explained I had just finished my Reiki master training, and while I developed more psychic abilities, I still wasn't having two-way communication with the spirit world.

I asked how he became involved in shamanism. Vague in his response, he said he had been going through "something." He did the usual therapy of peeling away layers but didn't feel any better or as if he had any answers. A friend suggested he see another friend, a shamanic practitioner. Then he became hooked.

As Michael explained, with shamanic work, messages and healing can come in the form of symbols and metaphors. One reason for this, he said, was if an answer is given literally, you think there is only one road you must take. But when spirits communicate using symbols and metaphors, you realize there are many possible paths, many levels of learning and meaning. By listening to a monotonous drumbeat when you "journey," it alters your brain waves, according to electroencephalographs (EEGs), so you can journey in an altered state of consciousness. In ordinary consciousness, our brainwaves are in beta state, he said. During drumming, the brain waves slow to alpha state, which is the beginning state of meditation. Then they slow even more to theta state. During the theta state is when we are in "non-ordinary reality" versus ordinary reality that we occupy normally. It's in this state that we encounter the spirit world where the shaman meets helping spirits (what mediums called guides) to work with the shamanic practitioner to bring healing to individuals, a community, and the environment.

He explained that, in shamanic beliefs, there are three worlds: the lower world, the middle world, and the upper world. The lower world would be where I'd meet my power animal and many other spirit helpers. The middle world is where we live, as well as the spirits of nature and living animals, and the upper world is where our spirit teachers reside. All of these worlds have many different levels. I wanted to go right to the upper world, but Michael said it's best to start in the lower world and meet my power animal, who would guide and help me on my path.

Michael picked up his drum and said that I could sit or lie down. I chose to recline on the couch. It seemed more, I don't know, therapeutic. He said to set an intent and mentally state it over and over. He instructed me to recite silently, "I'm going to the first level of the lower world to meet my power animal." I was to mentally go to a place in the ordinary world that I connect with in nature and look for an opening in the earth.

Here we go again with nature. Were all healers and mediums outdoorsy people? Maybe that was my problem. Why couldn't I go into a haunted mansion with Nancy Drew as my guide and look for the secret passageway in the library behind a moveable bookcase? After all, books were made from cardboard and paper, and cardboard and paper were once a tree. Wasn't that good enough?

While he drummed, I closed my eyes and did my best to imagine myself at my ancestral house in Ireland. I stood in front of the two-story, pale-yellow home with a center door and three chimneys. I surveyed the yard around it but didn't see anything that would give me access into the earth. So, I changed locales.

I scooted over to a fairy ring fort that Dwight and I had once visited in Ireland. There, I saw a tree with an inverted V-shape opening at the bottom of the trunk. I could see it at a distance of about a dozen feet or so, but for whatever reason, my mind would not let me go to it.

I now saw a hole in the ground. I watched myself sitting on the edge of the hole, but I couldn't bring myself to jump in. (Boy, was that symbolic or what?) Now I knew why I wasn't a fiction writer. I had no imagination.

The next thing I knew, without even consciously trying, I dove into the ocean—I wasn't even near the ocean in my mind—and swam down. It was mostly dark, although I could make out silhouettes of fish around me. I swam straight down. (Michael had said to go straight down, not at an angle.)

While I did this, I remained quite aware of my present surroundings. I heard Michael beating the drum, which was fairly loud for my liking, and I could hear when he stood up and brought the drum closer to me. I could also hear him moving around the room.

On my journey, I watched myself swimming down. I found it interesting that I viewed myself like a bystander. As some point, I must've made the "transition" that Michael had told me to watch for to the level of the lower world I was meant to be on. The ocean floor was wide open, all sand, no vegetation. I felt like I needed to sneeze, as if water had seeped into my nose. To the right, I saw a shipwreck. I couldn't see the whole thing, but the wooden ship looked like something Captain Hook might float out of.

I kept repeating my intention, and then a mermaid appeared out of the depths. At one point, we became one, but then she separated from me and swam ahead. I asked, "Are you my power animal?" But all I heard was "Follow me."

On my left, there appeared an orange-and-white-striped round fish. The mermaid kept swimming ahead of me, and I asked once or twice, "Where are we going?" The only answer I received was "Follow me," and she'd motion for me to follow. It didn't feel like we were moving, just suspended, even though I could see her tail moving up and down.

I wondered if she would tell me her name was Ariel, from the Disney movie *The Little Mermaid*, but her hair was not bright orange. It was blond. Then I wondered if she'd say her name was Lorelei, the name of the mermaid in *Beach Blanket Bingo*.

If you couldn't tell, I thought and analyzed the whole time.

As I tried to sort this out and follow the mermaid, the pace of the drum changed. Michael had said that this would be my cue to come back, so I said goodbye to her, swam straight up to the surface, came out of the ocean, and shook off my wet self.

Afterward, I told him about the journey. He thought I had done well for my first time. He said it's actually rare for a beginner to meet a power animal on the first try.

"But," I said, still wiping my watery eyes, "how do I know it wasn't all in my imagination? After all, a mermaid isn't real. How can that be my power animal?"

"Power animals can be real or mythological."

That made no sense to me.

Michael smiled. He was a patient, experienced teacher. "Power animals and spirits come to us in forms we can understand."

I nodded and wrote that in my notes, but thought, *I understand tigers. Why wasn't my power animal a tiger? I loved big cats.*

Several weeks later, when Michael finally said I could travel to the upper world, I was ecstatic. Here was my ticket to the magical mystery tour that would help me become a medium. You'll never guess who appeared as my teacher from the upper world. Athena. That's right. Another mythological being. I hadn't studied Greek mythology since seventh grade language arts class, so I had to look her up online when I arrived home. She was Zeus's favorite daughter and "the goddess of wisdom, courage, inspiration, civilization, law and justice, just warfare, mathematics, strength, strategy, the arts, crafts, and skill," and in more recent times, auto mechanics. (Okay. I made that part up, but seriously, she was probably the one who alerted us to the van transmission problem.)

Michael said the way to tell if a journey is "real" or "imagined" is to watch for synchronicities afterward. The next evening, as we watched *Jeopardy!*, there was a category on mythology. As soon as I heard it, I knew there'd be a clue about Athena: "This goddess of wisdom had an unusual parentage—no mom, just sprang full grown out of Zeus's head." Yep. That's my girl, Athena!

If like attracts like, I could understand why both a mermaid and Athena would come in those forms. They were manifestations of me. I came to realize that Mermaid signified my fun and playful side. Athena represented my wise, intellectual, and serious side.

On another journey to the upper world (I became an expert at taking notes while my eyes were closed), I swear to God, I met Jesus—white robes, long hair, beard, and everything White-Christian America thinks Jesus looks like.

"This is the level where the Christians come," he said. "I greet them. They're expecting me. On another level, there's Buddha or Mohammed or God. We appear in the image the person would recognize from their lifetime. There are even pearly gates, if that's what someone expects to see. We aim to please." He smiled. That's great. Jesus has a sense of humor.

He motioned for me to walk with him. He stopped and pointed. "That's where God sits, because people like to see God's throne."

I thought, *It feels like Disney World or some other amusement park, giving the person what they want to see.* Jesus responded to my thought, "We're okay with that. We just want them to get here; then we can help them learn what the afterlife is really about. This is the level after the life review. That's on the second floor. This is like third-floor lingerie." He smiled.

"Seriously?" I asked. I thought, *I must be making this up.* And he responded again to my thought. "And what if you are? The levels are what *you* expect them to be. For others, they are what they expect them to be. We don't care. We just want the souls to come to their 'heaven.' It's what will make them happy and bring them peace. And once they learn there's no judgment, it all falls into place for them—once we eliminate the fear, and make it fun, like an amusement park."

"So, you're like Mickey Mouse," I teased him. Jesus laughed. He's a pretty funny guy. I never knew. I thought, *But he's probably appearing in a way I can relate to, yes?*

"Yes," he said. "While the concepts of the afterlife are the same," he continued, "love, forgiveness, peace, happiness—the ideal image of those concepts are different for everyone. That's what we give them. The ideal."

Michael and I had agreed to meet every other week. My homework after my first visit with Michael and my first journey to the lower world to meet my power animal was to journey every day, as that would help me advance more quickly. Fair enough. But now I was torn. *Do I spend twenty minutes every day journeying or meditating?* I committed to journeying, figuring I wanted to get the full experience and see where it would lead me on my mediumship path.

I ordered a drumming CD after that first session with Michael, and I also looked in a book I had purchased a while ago, not even sure at the time why I needed it: *Animal Spirit Guides* by Steven D. Farmer, PhD, who was also a shamanic practitioner. Under "snake," one of the meanings read, "You're about to go through some significant personal changes, so intense and dramatic that an old self will metaphorically die as a new self emerges." When I looked up rattlesnake (the rattle part also had to be significant), one of the meanings was, "Anything you do now to heal yourself physically and emotionally will be the start of a major transformative cycle for yourself, one that will lead to greater benefits for you and your family and friends."

While Farmer didn't include mermaids, I found something online on a site for shamanic studies. For mermaids, it said, among other things, "Mermaids call us to the unknown, urging us to abandon what we are and to become something new."

Now, how bizarre was that to have two totally unrelated creatures show up, one in ordinary reality and the other in the so-called non-ordinary reality, with essentially the same message?

After each session with Michael, Jim and I went to dinner at one of our favorite restaurants in Emigration Canyon called Ruth's Diner. Ruth had opened her restaurant as a hamburger joint in 1930 in Salt Lake City, but when the building the diner was located in was scheduled for demolition, she bought a Salt Lake Trolley car, moved it to a recess in the side of the road at Emigration Canyon, and reopened it in 1949. It was an out-of-the-way location, but locals knew of it. Ruth's was even featured on Guy Fieri's *Diners, Drive-ins and Dives*, which we learned when an out-of-town couple sitting next to us told us they were here because they had seen the diner on the show. There was often a wait, despite an extra seating area built on the back of the trolley car and a large outdoor patio.

We always ordered the same thing. Jim had the gravied pot roast with extra mashed potatoes, hold the veggies, and a Coke, and I had an iced tea with lime and the salmon BLT, hold the B, with pesto mayo on a toasted ciabatta roll. Sitting in a booth, the clang of silverware and din of other diners' conversations filling the trolley car, I told Jim after the first class, "I'm supposed to reconnect with my power animal, Mermaid, and get to know her, ask her things like how do I communicate with her, what role she plays in my life, what she wants me to learn, how she can help me, and how I can honor her."

Jim took a bite of his pot roast. He didn't say anything. I waited until he swallowed and took a sip of Coke. Still no comment. I think he was as skeptical as I was about all this.

"What do you think?" I asked.

He said he didn't know, but if I thought it would help with my journey to become a medium, he was all for it. I said I didn't know either. "But," I added after chewing my bite of salmon sandwich, "it feels right for now, and it's certainly interesting."

At Ruth's after the session where I reported meeting Athena in the upper world and that she was one of my teachers, I asked Jim, "Don't you want to try journeying?"

"I'm kind of afraid to now. If you got Athena as a teacher, I'd probably get Deputy Barney Fife."

CHAPTER 20

Healing My Ancestors

A tranquil voice said in my ear, "You're not breathing. You need to breathe."

"I can't," I replied in my mind.

The voice repeated, "You need to breathe."

"I can't." I was suffocating, yet surprised I wasn't panicked. *My body has forgotten how to inhale*, I thought.

The voice replied more firmly, although still calm, "You're on your back. You need to roll over, so you can breathe."

"I can't move," I insisted.

Just then, the spell broke. I awoke, rolled over, gasped for air, and began breathing again.

Being an annoyingly overachieving student, I did my journeying homework faithfully once the drumming CD arrived. At least I could control the drum volume on it. I met with Michael every other week and reported on my progress. But something didn't feel right. My goal was to become a medium, not a Reiki master or shamanic healer. While

I understood that in helping others, we help ourselves, now into my second year of my quest, I didn't feel any closer to my destination. Was I wasting my time? I enjoyed the journey work, meeting with Michael, and learning more about shamanism, but it seemed like a splinter path, not one that would converge with the route I wanted.

A few months into my shamanic studies, it dawned on me: the reason for this part of my journey wasn't about me healing others, but about me healing me. While meditation had done wonders for my daily life, helping me not to worry so much, not to judge and criticize so much, and to have more gratitude, shamanism healed my soul.

Early in our classes, I shared with Michael that I had been diagnosed with sleep paralysis. This is a condition during sleep where your mind is awake but your body is not, and you're unable to move. In my case, it felt as if there were six lead dental X-ray aprons over my entire body, like I'd been drugged and in the deepest sleep possible, yet I remained aware of being awake, conscious, thinking. Not only was I physically paralyzed, but my respiratory system had also shut down. I exhaled, but my lungs had forgotten how to inhale.

The episode that brought me to a sleep doctor was not like the other times. I wasn't focused on getting oxygen back into my lungs. I had zeroed in on the proverbial white light I saw above me—not a corridor or long tunnel, just a vastness of brilliant white—and I took off toward it. My consciousness left my paralyzed body and lifted itself toward the whiteness.

"Someone" said something to me (I don't recall now what), but the soothing voice tried to coax me back into my body. I mentally responded, "Let's just see what happens."

I felt no fear, no sense of evil. I didn't experience the sensation of suffocation as I did on other occasions because I no longer occupied my body to feel any physical distress. The white light drew me upward, while "something" tugged me back down. I recalled thinking as my consciousness tried to depart once again, "Leaving your body is a lot of work."

During this tug-of-war, in which I was like a cat who couldn't make up its mind whether to go out or stay in when the door was held open, I also became aware that my body temperature dropped. A sheet, blanket, and quilt covered me. I wasn't cold like when you step outside in sub-degree temperatures without a coat but absolutely chilled externally and internally. As I attempted again to lift up toward the white light, I thought, *This is a lot colder than I imagined it would be. Shouldn't the light have a warm feeling to it?*

That's when the spell broke, and a heavy-duty, industrial shop vac sucked me back into my body.

I gasped and resumed breathing. Movement returned to my limbs, but I lay still, feeling the sensation of my blood circulating again and my body warming. My chest and lungs ached as if I'd been running at full speed. (I don't know how I knew that. The only reason I would run at all was if a bear chased me.)

The episodes occurred sporadically, a few times a year, with no identifiable trigger. There was no predicting when it would happen. The sleep doctor I consulted—the director of the Sleep-Wake Clinic at the University of Utah Medical School—said, "If you can tell yourself to move even a pinkie, it will break the spell." That's what he called it, "a spell." The medical consensus was these episodes usually happened when a person was either just falling asleep or close to awakening. Not for me. It happened two to four hours after I'd fallen asleep. The sleep doctor also said sleep paralysis is "idiopathic," meaning there is no identified cause. Or as Hugh Laurie playing Dr. Gregory House put it on the TV show, "Idiopathic means we're idiots because we can't figure it out."

Michael emailed me one day out of the blue: "I have been journeying to support you & was shown to consider some healing work for your sleep paralysis. Journey on this to see what your helping spirit says, if you are interested." I had forgotten I had told him about my sleep paralysis.

So, I journeyed to the lower world to have a chat with Mermaid. She didn't have any particular words of wisdom, but out of nowhere, I had a clear vision of a woman's face with her red hair slicked back. She was pretty, but I did not recognize her. All I could see were her eyes, forehead, and top of her head. The rest of her face was covered with green foliage. The vision lasted a split second, but was clear, whereas normally when I journey, everything is out of focus, as if I'm journeying, well, underwater.

I tried again the next day. I asked Mermaid who the woman was that I saw so clearly last night and what she had to do with my sleep paralysis. Mermaid led me to her cove, and we sat on the beach. I told her what I saw, and as I described the woman with her nose and mouth covered, the thought popped into my head, *My mother tried to suffocate me when I was little.*

Surely this was symbolic or metaphorical and not literal. My mother had brilliant red hair when I was born and was overprotective of me, her only child, not just when I was little but certainly when I was a teenager. That's when I'm sure she realized how little control she had over me. I couldn't wait to hear what Michael thought and what he received in his journeying.

Not surprisingly, Michael's journey was a lot more interesting than any of mine. Once we settled into his basement family room, I took out my notebook, and Michael shared what he received.

"I was shown an image of you," he said, "with a rope tied to your left ankle, which was tied to your mom's left ankle, and so on back through the female ancestral line."

I told him that's what we genealogists call the matrilineal or umbilical line. The rope "lineage" (my wording), Michael said, "went back to a woman who had some kind of great event that caused problems for each of her female descendants. In the image, this woman had the rope around her neck."

He paused. I took notes while he spoke, then looked up. I found it all fascinating.

"But I don't get the impression she had been hanged," he continued. "Only that she was the start of the problem."

"Interesting," I said.

"I'm actually surprised that the healing involved ancestral work, especially knowing you're a genealogist."

As a genealogist, I'm always "honoring" ancestors in one form or another, whether it's researching my own or my clients' and writing their stories.

Michael continued, "I wondered if it was a curse."

I wanted to say, "You're kidding, right? A curse?" but didn't.

"But I had the impression it wasn't," he said. "It was some event that happened in this woman's life that caused the problem that manifested in some way in each generation."

For me, I guess it was sleep paralysis, but for my mom, it may have been her chronic depression.

I was floored. I now told Michael about my sleep doctor's DNA study on sleep paralysis, although it never materialized due to funding. I also shared that I had written a book, *My Wild Irish Rose*, about my maternal ancestry. I knew all of my first cousins on my mom's and dad's side, so when I emailed each of them, asking if they'd ever experienced sleep paralysis, I quickly isolated the condition to my mom's side. Laurie, I discovered to my surprise, had suffered from it, and so has a female cousin. No one on my dad's side had any sleep issues.

Michael had me journey and ask about the first thing I needed to do to connect with the female ancestor who created the problem to heal the sleep paralysis. He said, "It may not stop the sleep paralysis. The healing needs to be done on a spiritual level. The root of the spiritual aspect of the sleep paralysis goes back to one event in that person's life. You'll need to heal each generation."

I looked at Michael as if his brains had fallen out of his head. "How do I do that?"

He smiled. "You journey on it."

Journey on it. The answer is always to journey on it. Honestly. Why can't they just tell me directly? Why must we go through all this? Just get me to the destination.

Michael picked up his drum where he had it propped against the love seat and stood. As he began drumming, I closed my eyes and set my intent with my question in mind, "How do I heal each generation?" By this point, I could journey sitting up, notepad in my lap, pen in hand, and write down everything as it happened with my eyes shut.

I swam down and journeyed to meet Mermaid. The number ninety-nine popped into my head. I asked what ninety-nine meant. Is it ninety-nine generations or someone born like in 1899? I heard "ninety-nine times."

"What should I do ninety-nine times?" If it had anything to do with a nature hike and hugging ninety-nine trees, Mermaid could count me out.

No answer.

When I returned to ordinary reality and shared the journey with Michael, he said the ninety-nine times may be a ritual of something that I have to do ninety-nine times. Good grief.

He suggested I make an altar and journey on what should go on the altar. He said the altar would be a way to begin healing the line by remembering and reconnecting with the line. He suggested I start by placing my family history book on the altar. Then I could add to it.

He suggested even more journeys to do for my homework:

- Ask who the original person and the original cause of the problem was in the line. (In my journey on this, supposedly she was someone fifteen generations back, but there wasn't historical documentation to go back that far in Ireland.)
- Ask about the event that triggered all this. (Like the Irish pirate queen Grace O'Malley, my ancestor was a wild woman for her time. No surprise there.)
- Ask what else should go on the altar.

With the advice I'd received from Mermaid, not only did my book *My Wild Irish Rose* go on the altar (a TV tray from Walmart I set in the corner of my living room) but also a continuously burning candle (battery-operated—I didn't want to burn down my house in the process). She also showed me a white rose. I bought an artificial one and put it in a vase. In another journey, she told me to keep the altar for ninety-nine days, so a little more than three months. That was reasonable. All I needed to do was dust it. And it would take me to about the end of my second year of this quest, which wasn't looking any more promising that I'd become a medium than when I started.

CHAPTER 21

There's a What in the Yard?

Winter solstice 2014 came along. I'd been studying, healing, and experiencing all sorts of interesting phenomena in those first two years, but I felt no closer to becoming a medium. While I had learned a lot about Reiki and shamanism, for which I was grateful, and I had grown a lot too, I wondered why all these rituals—smudging, lighting candles, buying crystals, setting up altars, and journeying—were necessary to mediumship. I had seen a good number of certified mediums, including Kim Russo, demonstrate at the afterlife conference. They didn't use any rituals. The room wasn't smudged. No one drummed. No candles burned. No one surrounded us with white light. We didn't meditate beforehand. And not a crystal vendor was in sight. The mediums just mentally connected with the spirit world. How did they do that? That's what I still needed to find out.

I decided it was time to wrap up my shamanic studies, so on a Friday evening during meditation, I asked the spirit world for a sign that my maternal line had been healed and I could move on.

The following Sunday, the winter solstice, started out like any Sunday morning. Jim worked downstairs on his computer, and I read and had tea in bed. The phone rang. When I answered it, our new next-door neighbor from Slovakia was in a panic. She didn't even say hello or identify herself.

"There's a big bird in the backyard! I don't know what to do!"

I said, "Hold on. I'm upstairs, and I can see into your yard."

I assumed it was a hawk. We've seen a lot of them flying around, and one even landed on our fence post one time. When I looked out the window, though, I didn't see a hawk. I saw a male peacock! It had perched on the fence between our yards.

I called down to Jim and told him there was a peacock on the fence. He grabbed his cell phone and took pictures. Then our frantic neighbor let her damn dog out and scared the poor thing away. It flew into the parking lot behind our condos. We don't know where it went from there, and we had no clue where it might have come from. The nearest zoo was fifteen miles away. All I knew for certain was I received my sign. It was too much of a coincidence to be a coincidence.

I just had to email Laurie the picture of the peacock perched on our fence. I hadn't told her about healing our maternal ancestry and asking for a sign. I still shared with her what I was doing, but not in as much detail. I no longer asked or expected any kind of validation. This time, though, she emailed back almost immediately: "Shut the fuck up! Uh, didn't think they were Utah natives. Perhaps an escapee. That's crazy!"

The crazy part hadn't even happened yet.

Laurie, her husband, Dash, and their toddler daughter had flown to Hawaii for the holidays to visit his family. Laurie was about six months pregnant with their next little girl. She emailed me the next day, "BTW, we saw a male peacock yesterday in Dash's mom's yard the same day you saw yours. Weird."

Weird?! Was she fucking kidding me?

I emailed back and asked if Laurie was toying with me.

"No! Dash and I were with Verity in the car leaving and it was right outside her front yard, in their long driveway-type road. It was just crossing, minding its own business. Dash told me to take a picture for you, but my camera was in the trunk. I swear!"

It was one thing for me to get a sign like this, but quite another for my daughter to also see a peacock on the same winter solstice, that time of year when darkness leads to light.

Did this change Laurie's mind? I wish it had. She considered it a spooky coincidence. But for me, I had no doubts. That we had both seen a peacock on the same day I took as a sign that the maternal line had healed both backward and forward down through my daughter, granddaughter, and unborn granddaughter.

I later looked up the symbolism for a peacock. One of the interpretations was "You're safe and very well protected, so there's no need to worry."

I guess so. More than seven years later, neither Laurie nor I have had any more sleep paralysis episodes.

CHAPTER 22

We're Off to
Spiritualist Camp

It had been two years and three months since I had decided to become a medium, and I'd yet to do a mediumship reading for someone. I didn't feel comfortable doing a reading for any friends. I knew too much about them. I needed people I knew nothing about.

In February 2015, we visited Cassadaga Spiritualist Camp in Florida. Located off the beaten path, Cassadaga was a quaint tourist town where all the residents are Spiritualist mediums, and street signs proclaimed, "Spiritualist Street" and "Mediumship Way." The rural community contained acres of land with seven parks and gardens. The town proper had colorfully painted Victorian-style homes and a bookstore with a gift shop. I couldn't resist the purple T-shirt emblazoned in white letters: *Got Spirit?* Strolling the main thoroughfare, we came upon a hotel, a building that housed meeting rooms and classrooms, and an assembly hall that doubled as a church. According to an article in *USA Today*, "Cassadaga was founded in 1894 by George P. Colby, who said he was led to the property by his Native American spirit guide, Seneca. The town was originally conceived as a winter residence for Spiritualists from Lily Dale, N.Y."

We were headed to Florida anyway to visit my dad in Orlando, and Cassadaga was just forty miles away. When I checked the Cassadaga website, I found three mediumship development classes offered during the two weeks we'd be in the Sunshine Disney State. The first one I attended felt like I'd walked into kindergarten class. We even did crafts with artificial flowers and cutout hearts since it was close to Valentine's Day, which was Jim's birthday, so I gave him my construction paper heart after class. Granted, the hearts were supposed to represent the love spirits send us, but still. The second class was how to do cold readings on people, and there's nothing psychic or mediumistic about it. The reader (also called a mentalist) tells a person about themselves based on how they dress, the jewelry they wear, generalized statements that can apply to practically anyone, and reading facial expressions and body language. "You have an hour with someone," the person teaching it said. "You have to talk about something." Good heavens.

That "class" was so disappointing I almost didn't go to the third one. Jim went with me this time. This class was held on a Saturday morning and conducted by Rev. Rob, who's the pastor of his own Spiritualist church and had studied at the Arthur Findlay College in England. I would later learn that the college is the premier school in the world for psychic and mediumship studies. Some say it was the inspiration for J. K. Rowling's Hogwarts school in the Harry Potter series.

The class was held in the church, the Colby Memorial Temple, in a large gathering area to the left as you walked in. The church looked like most any other with pews, pedestals with artificial sunflowers, a dais with a lectern, and chairs. There were no religious icons, only paintings of landscapes, angels, and sunflowers. The building smelled old, moldy, and musty, with floorboards that creaked when you walked on them.

We instantly liked Rev. Rob. A short, friendly man with gray hair, he came up and greeted us when we walked in. About a dozen or so students attended, and I heard someone say that there were a lot more people than last week. His classes ran weekly, but unfortunately, this would be the only one I could attend.

Our chairs were arranged in an oval, and after everyone settled in, Rev. Rob opened the class with a ten-minute guided meditation. We all stretched and resettled again, and then he said that memorizations of affirmations don't really work in developing mediumship. Ah, now this was the direction I'd been looking for.

"The spirit world will never send us fear," he said. "If you feel fear, that's your mind, and you need to move beyond it. Fear is the mind's reaction to the unknown or what we haven't experienced yet."

We learned that messages from the spirit world would never contain fear, such as a loved one saying they were "stuck" or "earthbound." No spirit is ever "stuck" or in need of rescuing. The spirit world welcomes everyone and is there when someone makes the transition. No one dies alone. The spirit world communicated messages about hope, healing, love, and upliftment.

I looked around the room. Everyone paid attention. Some, like Jim and me, took notes.

"Most of your teaching will come from spirit," Rev. Rob said.

Evidently, someone the week before had asked how you can tell whether you're getting something from spirit or it's your imagination. Rev. Rob gave the best explanation I've yet to come across. He said, "It *is* imagination, but *spirit-guided imagination*. Spirit takes a series of stored memories and combines them to tell the 'story' or the message. Spirit draws on common pieces of memory. You allow the imagination to work with spirit. Setting your intention also sets the vibration of receiving. If you think something doesn't feel right, that you're not getting it right, it probably isn't."

I liked his clear way of explaining things. He made it sound logical, not mysterious.

Rev. Rob mentioned the CERT method of mediumship: communicator, evidence, reason, and tying it up. Who is the spirit communicator? What is the evidence? Why are they coming through? And tying up the message. (I would later learn that this method has mostly gone out of favor with a lot of British medium teachers. Just let the spirit communicator talk and tell his or her story. They will give the evidence their loved one will recognize.)

When we took a break, Rev. Rob came over to us and asked what we thought so far. We told him we were visiting from Utah and here for only a few more days, so I was disappointed I couldn't take more of his classes. He said he puts his classes on YouTube, and I was welcome to view them there.

After the break, his students (mediums in training) did readings in front of the group. One said he had a message for "the man writing something in the notebook," and he pointed to Jim. Jim put down his pen, and I took up mine.

The pudgy medium with a beard and a lift on one of his shoes said a woman was with him, about "this tall," indicating with his hand that she was shorter than he. "She had a sense of humor once she got to know you. Once you get past her barrier, she's a vivacious spirit." Unlike Rev. Karen from the church in Vegas, he kept his distance and kept his eyes open.

Jim nodded in agreement. He thought it was his mother.

"She had circulation problems," the medium continued, "a heart condition and something in her lungs. Respiratory failure. She couldn't catch her breath."

I took notes so Jim could give the medium his undivided attention. He nodded again.

The medium added, "She says you did quirky things as a child. You can feel her presence. The relationship is so imprinted that you still do things as second nature. The bond is still close. She sends lots of love and continues to watch over you. She's still present and connected."

We thought he was finished, but then he added, "Oh, there's something about the radio. Song that was one of . . ." He paused and listened to the spirit. "It's a song that you heard recently that reminded you of her. You're very dear to her and still are. You have a lot of wisdom."

Jim validated everything the medium said about his mom, including the song, which he hadn't mentioned to me. I said to the group after the medium finished that today was Jim's birthday. Everyone nodded and smiled. They knew why his mother would come through with a message today.

After another student went, I raised my hand and asked if I could try it. My heart pounded so hard I thought it would leap out of my chest and fall onto the floor right in the middle of the group. I'd never been so nervous in my life. I'd spoken at genealogy seminars and conferences in front of hundreds of people, and I'd never been this anxious. Jim could see my hands visibly shaking. If I'd had tiny ball bearings in my hands, they would have shaken out and scattered all over the church. Jim put his hands over mine. I whispered to him, "It's now or never!"

Rev. Rob said he wanted another student to go next, then I could. He seemed rather surprised that I asked. I couldn't blame him. He didn't know me from Eve. All of those who went before me were on target based on the recipients' responses, so there was a lot of good energy in the room. Before each reading, as a group, Rev. Rob instructed us to send positive energy to the medium. He stood with each person, placing his hand on their shoulder and coaching them along. I loved his method.

When he called me up, he said to me as I walked toward him, "I don't know how you work."

"I don't know either!"

"Have you ever done this before?"

"No."

The class gave me a round of applause. Then he had them do a short meditation and said to send me energy and positive thoughts for a successful reading. Rev. Rob was probably hoping for some of that energy himself, since he didn't know me at all.

Rev. Rob stood on my left and coached me through the reading, whispering in my ear and keeping his hand gently on my left shoulder. He had a calm and soothing voice made for this kind of teaching. I closed my eyes, and he said to envision the spirit walking toward me. I tried to calm my nerves and open the beacon of white light into my crown chakra like one of the mediumship books I'd read said to do. I'd never been successful just seeing a spirit walk up, but I was damned if I didn't see one in my mind's eye walking up to me, coming in from my right side. Once I nodded that I had someone, Rev. Rob had me open my eyes and look around the room. "Who is the spirit here for?" *God, I don't know!* I looked around the room and zeroed in on a guy to my right wearing a purple shirt. Purple was my favorite color. Rev. Rob said his name was Charles.

I closed my eyes to tune back into the spirit. Rev. Rob asked what I saw now. I said, "It's a man in a hat, like a fedora. He has on a suit with a tie. I have the impression it's the 1940s time period."

"Good," coached Rev. Rob. "Ask him how old he was when he died or tell me how old he looks."

"Maybe forties." Then I said, "I'm hearing 'forties,' but I don't know if it's 1940s again or he died in his forties."

I paused briefly and said, "I'm hearing cancer, but then nothing else."

Rob said to keep going. The spirit man drew my attention to his shoes. "There's something about his shoes. He has black, shiny shoes. I don't know if he's proud of his shoes or he had a shoe store."

Then I said, "I'm hearing the Great Depression now, and . . ." Without realizing it until the words came out, I said, "Oh. It's a suicide," and I put my hand to my throat. I had the impression he hung himself, but I didn't say it because I had already blurted out "suicide," and hadn't worded it more tactfully.

Rob coached me again, asking me to ask the spirit why he was here. I said, "He wants to say, 'I'm sorry.' He hadn't meant for it to end that way." I actually felt this spirit person's sadness and sorrow. Jim told me later that my voice, face, and body language changed at that point. He said it was quite visible.

Rob asked if the message would be for Charles or someone Charles knows. Rob said, "Don't think about it, just go with your first thought." I wasn't getting anything at first; then I said definitely, "Charles."

Rob asked what the message was for Charles. I said, "The man sees him getting overwhelmed with everything, but don't get overwhelmed with everything like he did. There is a brighter future. He didn't see it, but there is a brighter future."

Then Rob said to tie it up, and I said, "The spirit wants you to keep moving forward and not give up."

When I finished, Rob and I both looked to Charles for validation.

"I'm sorry," Charles said, "but it doesn't ring any bells. Maybe it will in another day or two." But Charles admitted the message resonated with him.

Rob encouraged me, but as I took my seat, tears welled in my eyes. Jim patted me on the thigh. I had worked so hard for this. This was it. I wasn't a medium. I would never be a medium.

Rob said to the group that I had an even flow and constant communication, which shows a natural ability. He said my demonstration didn't come across as rehearsed or ritualistic.

How could it be? There was no natural ability. I had crashed and burned.

A guy a few seats away from Charles then spoke up. "My name is Charley or Charles," he said, "and my uncle was also named Charles. He committed suicide during the Depression. He was a very dapper dresser just like you said."

This Charles also wore a purple shirt but a different shade. When I stood to do my reading, he sat also to my right but behind me, out of my field of vision.

I wanted to get up and kiss him. My tears of disappointment changed to tears of relief. Jim beamed and patted me on my thigh again.

At the end of class, I talked to Charley. When I walked up, he was telling someone that his uncle had hung himself. I said, "That's what I got, but I had just blurted out suicide and didn't know how far to go with it." I realized he wouldn't have been able to see me put my hand to my throat when I did my reading. I asked if the message also resonated with him, and he said it did. So, I must have zeroed in on the wrong Charles.

We thanked Rev. Rob before we left, and I gave him a hug. He gave me his email and told me to keep in touch.

I was certainly on a high after my reading, and we hadn't expected that Jim would get a message. At our late lunch of birthday and celebratory steak dinners at Texas Roadhouse, Jim said even though he knew how nervous I was, he was proud of me for taking the risk. "Everything came through naturally, more naturally," he said, "than some of the students who did readings." I beamed a smile at him. He continued, "Rob didn't have to keep telling you to reconnect with the spirit or to step back and reconnect. Your pauses were shorter, and everything seemed really focused."

Jim has always been my "biggerest fan" and supporter, but I also knew he wouldn't just humor me. Not about this. He knew how important this was to me. I'd become a certified genealogist and had earned a master's degree, but this felt like an even bigger accomplishment.

"So, how has all this changed you?" I asked after taking a sip of my wine. Because we ate between the lunch and dinner crowd, the restaurant wasn't noisy, and they hadn't cranked up the country music too loudly yet.

"Well, as you know, I've always believed in an afterlife, but being raised Catholic, it was vague and theoretical. I always felt it was much more complex than the simple heaven or hell, salvation or damnation philosophy of my catechism and altar boy youth. With just the few readings I've gotten from my family so far, especially the one today from my mom for my birthday, the afterlife has become real." He took another bite of his baked potato and looked like he was pondering something else. "And it's proven to me that calling on my mom for help, rather than someone like Saint Anthony, the patron saint of lost things, is more likely to turn up my misplaced keys."

I laughed. Jim misplaced a lot of things. He probably needed the help of his mom *and* Saint Anthony.

"It makes me realize, too," he added, "that our time here isn't the end of anything. And it's not just about accomplishing things. It's about learning life lessons." Jim smiled at me. "I guess that's a good thing, because, for me, I've had more life lessons to learn than accomplishments."

"So true," I said and laughed.

As we enjoyed our steak dinner, I felt satisfied and even more driven. The past two years of my journey had finally paid off. I could indeed talk to the dead and have them talk back. I might be a medium after all. But the story wouldn't end there.

CHAPTER 23

My Self-Imposed Spirit Training Program

I was still on an emotional high after returning home from Cassadaga, and I reached a turning point with Laurie. While I was excited I had finally done a mediumship reading, I resisted the urge to share with her every detail of my journey. She worked full time, had a three-year-old, and gave birth to her second daughter the month after we came home from Florida. She was focused on life, not the afterlife.

As I continued to watch and study medium Kim Russo on *The Haunting of . . .* TV series, I realized the reason she was so good was that she did readings all the time. That's what I needed to do. I needed to practice, practice, practice, but I still had the problem of having no one to practice on. In one interview with Kim, she had said that before she hung out her shingle, she did one hundred free readings for people. That sounded fine to me. But where would I find one hundred strangers?

I decided to embark on a self-imposed spirit training program, plunging right into the deep end. I took Rev. Rob at his word that the spirit world is our best teacher. I emailed a friend on the East Coast and one on the West, both of whom I knew would be supportive and open to mediumship. I said I was developing as a medium and offering free telephone readings. If they knew of anyone who might be interested, please have them email me. My goal would be the same as Kim's: one hundred practice readings. But mine would be an even better learning experience since my sitters wouldn't be in person. With a telephone reading, I'd have no visual clues from the sitter and would know only a phone number and first name.

Once I hung out the "Free" sign, the volunteers came. I began my spirit apprenticeship in March 2015, more than two years into my quest. I did two to four readings a week, and sometimes two in one day. Most of the readings were painstaking. What should have been a fifteen-minute reading often took me an hour. I had many long, silent pauses as I waited for spirit to give me information. I really didn't know what I was doing, but I must have been doing something right. Based on my volunteer sitters' reactions and responses, I had a decent accuracy rate of anywhere from 75 to 90 percent.

For each phone reading, I lit a candle on my desk and gathered my crystals in a small bowl: rose quartz for unconditional love, amethyst for a sense of calm and clarity, and green aventurine for strength, confidence, and courage. I sat for a few minutes, mentally opening my crown chakra and imagining being surrounded by white light for protection. I talked to my spirit team, setting goals such as, "Please don't let me make a fool of myself." Then at the scheduled time I had arranged with the sitter, I called and introduced myself. Most people were grateful for the reading. There were exceptions—the one who did her laundry while on the phone with me and the one who walked her dog in a park with other barking dogs while I tried to connect with her loved ones in spirit.

Putting the person I called on speakerphone, I told the sitter I'd be recording the reading on a digital recorder and would later email the recording. I reminded the person I was "in training," and asked that the person not give me any feedback until the reading was finished. I just needed a "yes," "no," or "I don't know."

"But if your loved one gives us the winning lottery numbers," I teased, "we agree to split it fifty-fifty." Laughter always relaxed me.

Spirit wasn't messing around. They put me right to work. My first phone reading was with a mom whose teenage son had committed suicide. I didn't know that in advance, thankfully. This was one of the beauties of mediumship, but also one of the aspects I found so stressful. I never knew who would communicate or what that spirit person would want to say.

For this first reading, I knew only the sitter's first name, whom I'll call Jessica. Her son immediately came to me when I shifted my awareness to the spirit world as Rev. Rob had taught me. I closed my eyes and looked with my mind's eye to see who came walking toward me. (I later established with Team Sharon to have spirits come from behind, males behind my right shoulder, women behind my left. This way I could tell the difference between working mediumistically or psychically, when I would feel the sitter's energy from the front).

A young boy stepped forward, and I said he felt around ten but under fifteen. She said her son was a bit older than that when he passed. I said he might be showing a memory. Then I received a movie image in my mind of the boy on an Easter egg hunt. This was new for me. I'd never had moving pictures. I told her about the egg hunt, and that he was happily running around looking for eggs. She said it made sense. I then saw a little girl with him. She was in a blue dress, and they were hunting for eggs together. The mom said it must have been his cousin.

"Your son is looking for a large egg, not the smaller ones everyone else was gathering," I said. Jessica understood and told me later that the grandparents would always get a giant plastic egg and put a twenty-dollar bill in it. That was the prize egg. She also told me after the reading that she and her parents were talking recently about continuing the tradition of the Easter egg hunt this year.

I felt the young man had taken his own life, but I used the word "accident" instead. I didn't know how to delicately say, "He committed suicide," and I was also hoping I was wrong. But I didn't feel any sadness, regret, or remorse with him, and I told her so. His light and happy energy was in total contradiction to all I'd read and heard about suicide victims on the other side, so I knew I couldn't be making up these feelings. Jessica confirmed it was a suicide.

"It feels as if taking his life was all part of his soul's plan." She seemed to have instinctively believed this, too.

Jessica said he died a few months before our call when he was just eighteen. She told me after the reading that he loved watching all the ghost-hunter shows. I guess that's where he learned there was an afterlife, and he'd be able to communicate.

Jessica asked if her son had a message for his brother. I heard him say, "Stay strong." Then I received a visual image of a sliding glass door, which I sensed was symbolic for the other side. I told her, "He's just on the other side of that sliding glass door. He can see his brother, even though his brother can't see him. He's still with his brother, and all of you."

She emailed me afterward, saying, "It wouldn't surprise me that my son would try to push the suicide thoughts away. He was such a fun-loving guy and always making people laugh! The class clown. I just think that what he did was bigger than him. I cannot find it in myself to be angry with him, but I hurt because he was hurting. That younger age you mentioned was much more carefree and happy, and I do believe he was telling me to focus on those happy memories and to allow myself to smile about them instead of cry about them. He would not like me struggling like I am."

One reading about a month into my self-imposed apprenticeship stunned both me and my sitter, whom I'll call Imelda. As usual, I had only her phone number. No last name. I did my pre-reading ritual, then when I had Imelda on the phone, I began by saying that I saw a family gathering at an Italian restaurant, which she understood. Then

I heard the name Mario. I didn't always get names, but she said that her father's brother was named Mario.

Then a male stepped forward. "He was a short man," I described, "I'd say about five foot five, with thinning hair or balding, heavyset, and he wore reading glasses. I see him putting them on top of his head." Imelda said that it could fit for two men she knew who had passed. I felt like it was a father, and again she said it could be one of two men. She later told me that her father-in-law also met that description. I got a *C* name, later Charley. She was wishy-washy on that detail, but it wasn't the name of either.

In my mind, I asked the man for something he had left behind that Imelda might have. "He says you still have one of his shirts, and that you had recently taken it out and either looked at it or smelled it or wore it." She said yes. She later told me that she was down in the basement one day before our call and pulled out a work shirt of her father's that he'd left at the house and worn when he was doing repairs for her. That's when she was sure it was her father communicating.

Then, out of the blue, I heard "socket." I thought, *What?*

I said to Imelda, "This is going to sound really strange, but I just heard the word *socket*. Does that make any sense to you?"

She said yes, then I could hear her weeping. She later told me her immigrant dad was an electrician, and one time, he sent her to the hardware store to get some "socket breakers." He meant circuit breakers but didn't know the right English term. Imelda didn't know any different, so she went to the store asking for "socket breakers." That became a running joke in the family and between them.

Her father showed me his headstone and flowers around it. I said, "You or someone recently put flowers at his grave, correct?" Then she told me the headstone is supposed to be delivered and placed this week. I said, "He's happy with it."

Not all of my readings went that well. Three or four were total bombs, where the sitter didn't recognize the spirit communicator I had with me. Although I wasn't charging for the reading, which took some of the pressure off, I still wanted to do well for them and for myself. Those few sitters were understanding. If they were open to trying again, I rescheduled another reading. The second time always went much better. Who knows why. I learned that, for some readings, the energy just wasn't right, whether it was my energy, the sitter's, or the communicator's. The stars just didn't align for that reading.

Regardless of the off readings, word traveled fast about my offer to do free mediumship readings. I told each sitter to spread the word, and if someone wanted a reading with me, to pass along my email. But it was important that they tell any friends to give me only their first name and phone number, nothing more. I would set up a convenient time for the phone reading through email. I didn't want anyone thinking I was looking people up online or on Facebook.

By May 2015, I was up to thirty readings, and my thirtieth was another memorable one. I brought through Cindy's (not her real name) mom. The woman felt rather timid coming through, but I saw her as in her thirties, slender, and with light-brown hair. Cindy confirmed this. I tried for her name and got Gloria or a *G* name. Her name was Rochelle. I'd need to work more on names. Sometimes I'd nail them; more often I didn't.

I felt as if Cindy's mom did some kind of work outside the home and wore makeup and had her hair styled. Cindy said no. I tried not to let the "no" responses bother me, but, of course, they did. Back then, I didn't know to give one piece of information at a time, then get validation. Was she saying no to her mom working outside the home or wearing makeup and having her hair styled?

Then I said I saw the woman in a nurse's uniform and asked if her mom was a nurse. She said she was. So, she did work outside the home. Whew!

A bit later, Cindy's mom brought up the makeup again. I said,

"Your mom is mentioning the makeup again, and now I hear the word *Avon*. Did she sell or buy Avon?" I could hear Cindy sniffling. Yes, her mom had sold Avon when Cindy was a toddler. After that, I knew the reading would go well, and I learned that if something was important, the spirit person would bring it up again.

It was an hour-long reading, with a few more misses but a lot more "hits." As I concluded the reading, I always asked the sitter if they had any questions they wanted to ask their loved one. Cindy started sniffling and crying again. She said she still feels so guilty, and she wants her mom to forgive her. Cindy didn't go into detail, which was fine with me. I didn't want it to cloud my reading. But as she spoke, I saw her mom gather in her arms a big bouquet of flowers that she wanted to give Cindy as a symbol of her love and forgiveness. I couldn't tell what all the flowers were, but I could see there were some kind of pink lilies in the bouquet. "Calla lilies," I said, the name finally coming to me. I heard Cindy gasp and sob more. As it turned out, Cindy's mother had passed eight years ago, but she still carried guilt with her over something she felt she needed her mother's forgiveness for. She found it difficult to speak after the reading, but she emailed afterward:

"Sharon, I am actually feeling as if a giant weight has been lifted from my heart. Here is a picture of me at our wedding. My favorite flower is the pink callas in my bouquet. I am torn up emotionally, but I wanted to send you this picture! Thank you so much!"

I didn't understand how profound and powerful the messages and presence of our departed loved ones could be until that moment.

In September 2015, approaching three years to the time of my journey's start, I hit that goal of one hundred free readings. I was happy with how my mediumship progressed, but I knew I needed a mentor or some classes. The information still came to me terribly slowly and in random bits and pieces. Kim Russo's readings weren't anything like that.

I'd seen her work live when we went to the Forever Family conference. There were no long pauses with her. If only she offered classes. But she didn't, and anyway, I was far from New York where she lived. I went back online. Surely Google, my spirit guide in the cyberworld, would help me. As they say, when the student is ready, the teacher will appear. I was ready!

CHAPTER 24

Finally, Some Mediumship Classes

I had become aware of the Spiritualists' National Union in the UK during my search for information about mediumship, but what I hadn't stumbled upon yet was their online international branch: SNUi, or the Spiritualists' National Union International. They offered not only online classes and services but also an accreditation and certificate program I could do online. Now, this was what I was looking for! I joined immediately in October 2015 and began to attend every class on mediumship development they offered in my time zone. Because they were located in the UK, many classes were held in what was the middle of the night for me. I was dedicated, not crazy.

I took weekly online classes with Margaret Challenger from Wales, a certificate holder in mediumship of the parent organization, the Spiritualists' National Union (SNU). She'd been a medium since the age of two, and her mother was a medium. Boy, was she lucky.

At the time, the SNUi used an online meeting platform called MegaMeeting. There was no video, only audio, so I couldn't see Margaret, and she couldn't see me or any of the other attendees. All anyone could see was the person's first name in the user's box. This didn't bother me since my practice readings had been done "blind" over the telephone. Students from around the globe attended Margaret's Mechanics of Mediumship classes held every Thursday. Usually more than two dozen came to her workshops. It was nothing short of amazing that I could sit at my desk in front of my laptop in Utah at eleven in the morning, while Margaret sat in her home in Wales at six in the evening, and we could both be connected to the same person in spirit, in their world without time zones.

Margaret was a tough teacher who insisted on discipline in mediumship. She had high expectations of her students, which I liked. And she had a wonderful sense of humor. Her laugh was more of a giggle and so endearing. I felt drawn to be in her presence, and after my first class with her, I vowed never to miss one. I knew I would learn a lot from her. I later saw a picture of her on Facebook: her smile sparkled in her eyes, and she radiated her soul's beauty.

When I attended her classes, it was helpful to simply listen to her answer questions and coach the other students. It surprised me when she called on me during the first class I attended. She said she let spirit guide her, and she felt drawn to me. "What questions do you have?" she asked.

It was a good thing she couldn't see me. I'm sure my mouth dropped open to my chest, and my cheeks burned.

"Well," I said, "the information seems to come in slowly for me."

"I know exactly what you're talking about," she said. "What happens when you do a reading and get yeses is you don't feel like you have to work as hard. But when you get a no, then you have to work harder." That was true. The "no" response, although I knew that no medium was 100 percent accurate, always threw me. When it happened, it dropped me out of the contact, I went into my head, and I had to "work harder" to reconnect with the spirit person.

As if she'd read my mind, Margaret said, "When you're thinking, you're not linking." That would be a mantra I would hear many times in classes with her.

Then, out of the blue, she said, "You have a woman standing there in front of you. If you put out your left hand, you could touch her. Do you see her?"

Shit! I was not expecting that!

I closed my eyes, and I saw in my mind's eye a lady standing there. Was I imagining it? Perhaps it was the power of suggestion. Margaret asked me about the woman's build. I said, "She's average build, not heavy, not thin, and of average height, which, to me, is around five foot five or six."

"Now move your energy into hers," Margaret directed, and I imagined my energy moving outward.

"She's come closer," I said.

"Does that surprise you?"

"Yes."

"Why?" Margaret asked.

I didn't have an answer but again wondered if this was all the power of suggestion.

Margaret said when she moved her energy into the woman, she bumped into her large bosom, and said to the spirit, "My, you have a large bosom!" I didn't see that at all. But I liked Margaret's sense of humor and how she spoke to the spirit person.

Then Margaret asked me to describe her eyes. I said they were brown and warm. She asked me if they were bright and sparkly. I said they were, but again, I was concerned that I saw this because Margaret had asked me that question. That didn't seem to faze Margaret. She asked me to tell her something else about the woman's face. I said, "Her lips are pursed, and I feel like she's annoyed."

Margaret said, "Good. Why is she annoyed?"

I paused a moment. "I feel like she was annoyed because she wasn't being heard."

Margaret then threw me another curve ball. "Who has she come for?"

Oh God, I thought.

"Scroll down the list of names, and say the one that lights up," Margaret continued to coach me.

I took my mouse and scrolled down the list. The name *Andy* stood out to me, so I said his name.

Margaret called on Andy and asked if he could take the information. He said it sounded like two people he knew. She came back to me and asked me to give more information.

"She has her hand on her hip, like she's impatient. She's drawing my attention back to her lips. They're pursed because she was a smoker."

When Andy couldn't understand the smoker piece, I told Margaret that maybe I had picked the wrong person from the list. She said, "No, the woman is definitely here for Andy."

She asked me who the spirit was, what her relationship was to Andy. I said, "A mother or someone like a mother." Margaret said, "Why *or*?" I didn't have an answer for that. She said, "Just say 'mother.'"

She asked me who else the mom was bringing in. I said, "She's grabbed someone by the hand and is pulling in a man. It feels like he doesn't want to be here. He's reluctant to come in."

Margaret rephrased it: "Andy, do you recognize a man who's rather shy who'd be with your mum?" Yes, he could. "There you go," she said to me.

I was learning the language of spirit, and that communication with them should be like having a conversation. She likened it to being in a room and getting a phone call for someone's "mum." You'd call out and say, "Andy, I've got your mum here. She wants me to tell you this and this. And, oh, do you know what she's showing me now?"

The other suggestion she offered was not to interpret what you're getting. Just give what you get. She said spirit communication is all about the emotion. Give the emotion you receive. And remember, she said, "The communication is not for you. It's for the recipient."

Her workshops were hard because I had to maintain the contact with the spirit while she was coaching me or calling in the recipient to ask if they understood it. It felt like the epitome of multitasking, but it taught me how to stay in the energy of the spirit. I also felt self-conscious that day because all the other students listened to her coaching me. Thank heavens all they knew was my first name, and they couldn't see me. That said, everyone was supportive. Several students wrote in the chat window that I had done a good job.

During the many months I attended her workshops, she drilled into us that the "language of spirit is emotion," to "give what you get," and most importantly, to "do as you're told." The spirit knows what their loved one will understand. We usually get a "no" because we add our own interpretation to what we receive.

As the classes went on, I also learned how to work more quickly and reduce the length of my pauses. I found if I kept talking by starting a sentence, any sentence—"He also wants you to know that . . ."—the spirit would finish the sentence by putting a thought in my head. I realized, too, from Margaret's classes that my mediumship really lacked discipline. My phone readings were all over the place. I gave bits of information here and there, but my mediumship wasn't consistent, and it didn't tell the spirit's story.

"Look at their hands," Margaret would instruct. "You can tell a lot about a person's life from their hands." Indeed, you could. A wedding ring indicated the spirit communicator was married. Rough, weathered hands indicated the person worked with their hands outside. Polished nails could mean that the woman didn't do much with her hands. Blistered palms could mean the communicator worked with heavy tools.

"Spirit people are intelligent," Margaret said. "They will give enough information to be recognized, then just let them talk about what they've come to say. Always remember," she told the class, "the communication is between the spirit person and the recipient. It's not for you. Stay out of it."

I took classes from other SNUi instructors, too, and asked one, "If I were ever to go to the Arthur Findlay College in England, who should I study with?"

Without hesitation, she said, "Paul Jacobs." She said some people don't like him because he's tough, but that's exactly why she liked him. I wondered how much tougher he could be compared with Margaret. She was tough! The other teacher warned me, "He doesn't hand out praise."

I would discover later when I took his workshops that a comment such as "I'm happy with that," after a student demonstrated in front of the class, was about the best praise students would get from him.

Paul had been one of five mediums mentored by Gordon Higginson (1918–1993), generally considered the greatest Spiritualist medium of the twentieth century. Gordon could give the spirit communicator's name, phone number, address, and other amazing details that only the spirit and their loved one knew.

I didn't expect I could afford to go to England for the Arthur Findlay College, but I saw on Facebook that Paul was offering a five-day progressive workshop in Southern California in March 2017 (a bit more than four years after I started my journey), and three additional workshops the following October, then the following year in March and October 2018. I couldn't pass on that opportunity. He was taking only sixteen students, so there would be individualized attention.

Jim and I drove from Salt Lake City to Norco, California. During the two-day drive, I chattered endlessly the whole way, wondering what the class would be like, who would be there, and whether I'd be the worst medium there. At one point, I asked Jim, "Why haven't you ever wanted to become a medium?"

"I've seen all the time and effort you've already put into your development. I never felt like I had that kind of discipline or enough time left in this life to do that."

He was right. I had put a lot of time, effort, and money into this journey. But it was paying off. Like genealogy, mediumship had become my calling. I couldn't not do it.

We spent the first night of the trip at the Tuscany Hotel in Las Vegas, and the next morning, as we walked through the outdoor plaza to the restaurant for breakfast, a song came over the loudspeaker that I had been using to raise my energy before I did readings or attended SNUi classes. It was Bruno Mars's "Uptown Funk." Why I picked that song, I had no idea. I liked the energy. But when I heard it, I took it as a sign that the workshop would go well.

The next day, when I entered the hotel conference room where the workshop would be held, the chairs were arranged in a semicircle with two chairs in the center front. Many of the other students were local and seemed to know each other, so I felt grateful when a woman about my age with long, blond hair came and sat next to me, then introduced herself. Susan was a practicing medium, but she was also an English teacher, as was I. We immediately hit it off and made plans to have lunch.

Paul Jacobs came into the room, dressed in a button-down white shirt, a black cardigan V-neck sweater (buttoned up), and light-blue skinny jeans. He wore a pair of reading glasses around his neck, but oddly, the frames must have had a magnetic nose piece, as they dangled open like a stethoscope. In his hand was a Styrofoam cup of coffee. He sat in one of the two chairs in the center of our semicircle, then waited for us to take our seats and become quiet. It reminded me of my high school, where some teachers sat silently and patiently for everyone to settle down.

He asked us to go around the room and introduce ourselves. "I don't want your life story," he said. "I just want to hear a little about your mediumship." *He knows what he wants*, I thought.

After the introductions, he continued to sit in the chair and gave us a lecture. Most took out notepads and wrote down everything he said. "Mediumship is a soul-to-soul blending. We have to be comfortable with our real self. This is all the spirit world has to work with.

"You can do a whole communication without seeing or hearing anything," he stated. "We cannot separate the clairs; all of them work together. The communication is a feeling first; then it will manifest in the other clairs. Once you receive an image, you should 'swallow' it and 'digest' it through the feelings.

"We feel the spirit first. Physical description is not a good way to start a contact, as it's often too vague and general anyway."

This was different from what Margaret taught. She encouraged giving physical description first, but ideally something unique about the physical appearance.

"Give only three pieces of information to start," he continued.

"There should be only one person who understands it if the information is specific enough. Yes?"

Focused on writing in our notes, we nodded.

"Yes?" he repeated. We shouted, "Yes!" "Good," he said. "Sometimes I think it's easier to talk to the dead." We murmured chuckles, and he smiled back at us.

"Mediumship is like a cut, polished diamond. We're working on only one facet of that diamond at a time in the workshop."

Paul said that the only questions we should be asking of the communicator are "Who's there? Who are you here for? What do you want to say?" Margaret taught basically this same thing. She said to think of it as spirit knocking on your front door, and what you would say when you opened the door.

This all made sense to me, and I was so happy to be in his class. We took a break, then for the rest of the day, he had us come up to the front of the room one at a time to do a short "dem," or demonstration of mediumship. Although nervous, I was actually grateful to see how the other students worked. Our group consisted of mostly women, only two men. It put me a little more at ease to see the variety of mediums, from beginners to advanced. I fell somewhere in the middle. But I put my mind to learning and not comparing. I was there to learn, not to show off. As if I could!

When it was my turn, I could feel my hands quivering and my heart thumping. But I used all that I'd learned on SNUi, connected with spirit, and said with confidence, "I have a father here who did woodworking."

Paul said, "And who do you feel drawn to?" I looked around the room. He said, "No. You don't look. You feel who you are drawn to."

So, I felt and pointed to a student. The student understood a father in spirit who did woodworking. But then Paul added to my comment, "Do you understand a father who did woodworking on model boats?" He got a strong "Yes!" I was learning to give all the details I had received. I had seen in my mind's eye a boat but said just woodworking.

During the five days, we did a variety of exercises, working specifically on clairvoyance (clear seeing) and clairsentience (clear feeling). We demonstrated in front of the class and in small groups, and we were paired with another student to do readings. For another exercise, half of us would stand facing the wall, and when we were told a person was behind us, we gave a reading to that unknown person, who would tap us on the shoulder once for "yes" and twice for "no." In between practice sessions, Paul gave more short lectures. I left the five days exhausted but invigorated, counting the days until the next workshop.

Paul Jacobs and Margaret Challenger were each the kind of tutor I'd been searching for. Teachers who didn't just tell me I did a good job, but who instructed me on how to keep improving. Mediums who connected with the spirit world naturally and without all the ritual and superstition of candles, crystals, smudging, opening and closing my third eye and chakras, drumming, or feeling the need to protect themselves. Their teaching was not fear-based. They both taught that people in the spirit world are just that: people. You talk with them as you would talk with anyone here in the physical world. Sure, they may communicate their sadness and regrets, as well as offer apologies, but this was part of their own healing journey.

Later, a real highlight of my training and development came when each of these two tutors asked me to share the platform with them and give public demonstrations (dems). With Margaret, my first dem with her was online on SNUi in March 2017, not long after my first workshop with Paul. (Two years later, I would have the exhilarating opportunity of demonstrating with her on the platform in her home church, Treforest SNU Church in Pontypridd, Wales. Her dems were amazing and inspiring. I felt mesmerized watching her as she radiated spirit's energy and her own.) For the online dem, I was to give two demonstrations of five minutes each. Margaret started by giving her demonstrations, then she called me in. Once again, I was happy no one could see me shake or sweat. I went to a woman named Maggie and brought her mom through. I didn't get a lot of cold, hard facts, but Maggie understood everything I said about her personality. For my second demonstration, I went to someone named Monica, and I brought through her stepfather, who I said was a dad. Again, not any real cold hard facts, but she recognized him from my description, the personality, and the memories he gave through me. I knew I needed to do more work on the "practical" information, as Paul would say. The concrete facts.

In the midst of all my training, an email from Laurie appeared in my inbox: "Your granddaughter made this at school. They were allowed to paint anything. She said it was a 'ghost woman.' Anyone you know?"

My granddaughter was six at the time, the age when many children become aware of the spirit world. I was beyond excited. Laurie said it was the first time she'd drawn a portrait of someone (usually she draws stick figures). No, I didn't recognize the crude watercolor painting, but it was definitely eerie. The lady's white, almost Albert Einstein hair was splattered with yellow and blue, her almond-shaped eyes painted yellow, half of her face painted purple, one arm red and the other yellow, and blue over her chest, more heavily over the heart. I had learned in Paul Jacobs's class on color readings that blue was typically the color for communication. What was she trying to communicate through her heart? And what was the emotion on the face? It looked like shock or surprise. My granddaughter painted the mouth open, in a circle, also yellow. The nostrils showed, not just a nose, as if the opened mouth had pulled the nose downward and caused the nostrils to be visible. The ghost woman looked like a female version of Edward Munch's 1893 painting *The Scream*. Laurie said that my granddaughter wasn't afraid of the woman, but the woman clearly seemed frightened or surprised by something.

I hadn't responded to the painting right away because Laurie's email had gone to my old email account. When I saw it three days later, it struck me as interesting that Laurie had sent it on Jim's seventieth birthday, Valentine's Day. Was there something shocking about his birthday? Of course, maybe I was reading too much into it, but as I'd learned, there was no such thing as a coincidence.

When I finally responded to Laurie, she wrote, "I was afraid that you hadn't responded because you thought I was mocking you . . . but I wasn't!"

I knew Laurie thought it was just my granddaughter's imagination, but she did admit it was weird. Perhaps this was the start of my granddaughter's "special abilities."

I did a public demonstration with Paul when I had invited him to come to Salt Lake City and do a workshop here in September 2018. By that time, I had completed three 5-day intensive and progressive workshops with him and would attend my fourth in October. I was also leading and teaching my own circle locally, giving small, public demonstrations with my students to audiences of about twenty, and I had passed my assessment for an accreditation as a platform medium with the SNUi in March 2018.

Jim helped me plan and coordinate the workshop and demonstration, arranging for the hotel and taking care of all the endless details that go into such an event. The conference room was set up with half the chairs on one side of the room, a narrow center walkway, and the other half on the other side. We told the hotel that we wanted about ten feet of space in the front and away from the audience, where two chairs were set out for Paul and me. We didn't use a dais. About fifty people attended the demonstration. Paul, in his navy-blue blazer and white button-down dress shirt, counseled me outside the room before we started. "Pretend I'm not here. Most students are more nervous because I'm on the platform with them." I smiled and said, "Don't worry. I plan to ignore you." He looked surprised but smiled back.

Paul opened the Evening of Mediumship with a short introduction, then did the first three demonstrations. He had told me to get my first spirit contact as he was finishing up his third, so when it was my turn, I'd immediately be ready to speak. He introduced me. I stood in front of the audience in a black-and-red, well-fitted, horizontal-striped sweater and black slacks, smiled, and welcomed everyone. I was even having a good hair day.

My hands still trembled, and my heart did somersaults, but I had learned that my nervous energy could be utilized and blended with the high vibration of the spirit energy, so I didn't let it bother me. By now, I trusted my spirit team and knew they wouldn't let me down. They wouldn't leave me standing up there, looking like a fool. I had made clear to them that I'd quit! I stood in the middle of the imaginary stage. My training had taught me not to venture into the audience as Kim Russo and the Forever Family mediums did. It was too easy to get pulled into the recipient's energy and to unintentionally do a psychic reading.

"I have an uncle here," I announced confidently. "He was either a pain in the neck or had a pain in the neck." I moved my body to the right where I felt drawn to a woman in the audience. "The lady in the blue sweater," I said and motioned toward her. "Do you recognize this gentleman?" She said she did, but it sounded more like her father. Again, Paul had taught that if you're going to be off on anything, it's most likely the relationship. I moved toward the right side of the room where she sat but made sure I was still visible and heard throughout the room. My years as a genealogical public speaker had taught me that.

The spirit communicator led me into talking about how he built his own television set. "It was a Heathkit," I said. The lady said it was. "Your dad says he also did TV repair on the side." She smiled and said he did. "He shows me he had one of those big caddies to carry tubes, correct?" She said yes. "And he talks about having schematics to repair different TV sets." I was nailing it. "Oh, and he says you sometimes helped him," I said. "You held a mirror in front of the screen so he could see what the picture was doing." Yes.

This reading came naturally for me. I didn't have to think about it, just follow the spirit's lead. My dad had been a TV repairman in the 1960s before he went to flight school, so this communicator could easily give me practical evidence that the lady could understand and accept. I had learned that spirit uses our own frame of reference for information, and that's why some communications flow and seem so easy. Spirit communicators work with our spirit team, so they know which medium to go to who will have that needed frame of reference for the communication. A spirit who loved football would never come to me. I didn't know a goalie from a goal post.

When I felt that the communicator had delivered his message and said all he needed to say, I moved back to the center of the "platform" and further away from the audience to "break the link." I took a sip of water, then connected with another spirit. My second contact was for a lady in my practice circle who was on the left side of the room next to her husband. I recognized her grandmother's spirit because I had brought her through before in our practices. I mentally asked the grandmother to give me information she hadn't given me before, and she delivered.

"Your grandmother grew a vegetable garden, correct?" I received a positive response but didn't need it. This piece, I had remembered. But then the grandmother gave me new evidence. "She mentions carrying in fruits and vegetables in her apron." I mimed looping up the bottom of an imaginary apron and placing fruits and vegetables in it. "Yes." "She says how she enjoyed making holiday meals for the family and putting out her china." "Yes." "She says you have her china." "I do." "She shows me the pattern has a gold rim and blue flowers on it." "That's right." "Your grandmother says you still have a large platter of hers that belongs to the set." "Yes." "And it's in a cabinet just collecting dust!" Everyone laughed, and she nodded. "She wants you to clean it and use it."

For my third contact, I said, "I have someone's boyfriend here. You and he used to date, but the romantic relationship evolved into a friendship." I turned my body to the right and felt drawn to the woman next to the one whose dad repaired televisions. "Do you understand who I have here?" She said she did. "He says that you still have his photograph framed in your bedroom on a dresser."

"Yes."

I smiled and laughed. "He says you also turn it facedown when you, ah, 'entertain company.'"

Both she and the audience laughed, and she confirmed that's exactly what she does.

I said, "He says he really enjoyed going to the movies." She said yes. The spirit gave me an image of the movie poster for *Jaws*. I said, "Oh, you saw *Jaws* together." No one was more shocked than I when she said yes. I could see mouths dropping open among the audience.

I looked at Jim, who stood at the back of the room. He gave me a huge smile and winked, then gave me the thumbs-up. I felt as if I'd arrived. It wouldn't get much better than this. When I sat down, I looked at Paul, and he smiled at me. I already knew not to expect any praise from him, so when he said to the class the next morning, "Sharon did very well last night," it surprised me.

But that evening of the demonstration, as I drove home, it hit me. I can actually converse with people who have died. Me. A nearly sixty-two-year-old woman. How amazing is that? It seemed nothing short of a miracle. But now it had become an everyday miracle.

Once home, Jim told me he had run into Paul in the hotel lobby when he went to take down the signs promoting the demonstration.

"Are you proud of your wife?" Paul asked.

Jim said he was.

Paul grinned. "You should be."

Epilogue

My mother had become quite the spirit communicator. When I joined the SNUi, I attended one of the online services with no video, only audio. The first medium doing a demonstration, Nadine, was from the Netherlands. "I have a woman in spirit with me," she began, "whose medical treatment had made her really sick, but she had tried to hold on and wait for her daughter to arrive before she passed. Can anyone take this information?"

I pressed my indicator button. I was the only one who did.

Nadine went on to say, "She had a long period of illness, and it really affected her belly." I said, "Yes." Mom had internal bleeding from the new blood thinner they had given her, and she was vomiting "coffee grounds."

Nadine continued, "The woman kept losing consciousness, but she kept trying to come back for her daughter." I said that was correct. The nursing home director, who sat with my mom until the end, had told me that Mom was in and out of consciousness until the last few hours. She was trying to hold on until my arrival.

Nadine said there was a lot of weakness, and that the woman had fallen down at some point. "Yes." Mom fell down a lot.

Nadine also said the woman had a problem with her right eye toward the end, but I couldn't confirm that. "She had some kind of cancer condition." I said no, but I could understand how a medium might think that given her symptoms.

Nadine then said, "She was a sweet lady." I laughed and said, "Well, that's debatable, but yes." Of course, if you look at it from Mom's point of view, she would have called herself a sweet lady.

Nadine said, "Your mother became more brave toward the end, and you were an important reason for her braveness. Being brave is something you have a lot of, more than her, and you should find the strength in you to continue to be brave." I suspected Mom meant her struggles with mental illness and having to raise me on her own.

Over the years, my mother has "come through" many times while I've sat in development circles or attended Spiritualist services. Her messages for a long time were ones of apology. When I meditated, I sent her apologies for the horrible daughter I'd been. Eventually, her apologies stopped, and so did mine. We forgave each other and ourselves and healed our relationship.

Mediumship, I learned, wasn't just about talking with the dead. It was about healing—for those on both sides of the veil. My quest to become a medium had unexpected bonuses: I resolved many of my unhealed wounds. Now I could provide healing to those in spirit as well as to those grieving the loss of their loved ones. This journey wasn't just about me anymore.

Joining SNUi and training with UK mediums were the steps most instrumental in my mediumship development. I realized there was a big difference between British mediumship teachings and American mediumship teachings, which tended to be more "New Age." Several American mediums, in my experience, teach fear of the spirit world, and that you need to perform rituals, such as opening chakras, smudging, and constantly protecting yourself, or that you need to use the "tools of the trade," such as candles and crystals. That's what happened when I started this journey. Fear kept me from making a move unless I did or had all these things. (If they happen to float your pirate ghost ship, and you're using them simply because you like them, that's fine. But know they aren't necessary.)

When I joined SNUi and started learning from British mediums, I discovered there is nothing to fear from the spirit world. Like attracts like. If your intentions are good, then that's what you will attract. Connecting with the spirit world is natural. Anyone can do it. You don't need any props or rituals. But not everyone will put in the effort to properly train and develop with the necessary discipline.

I also learned from the British Spiritualist teachings that there is no need to know who your spirit guides are, how many there might be, what their names, ranks, or serial numbers are, or what purpose they serve in your life. Just trust that they are there and listening. They don't care what you call them. They have ascended to a level beyond the ego. The important thing is to think of them as your new best friends and talk to them. Invite them to help you in whatever area of your life you need. Some people prefer to go straight to God or an angel, and that's fine. But God or an angel may be delegating a spirit guide to assist you. According to Spiritualists, spirit guides serve a specific purpose in the cosmos, and that is to work with and guide the living.

I hadn't been looking for a religion when I started this quest, but I found one that resonated with me. I converted to Spiritualism. Even though Spiritualism is an American-born religion, brought to England by an American medium, Maria B. Hayden, a woman about whom I would later write the definitive biography, the British Spiritualists and their philosophy spoke to me more than the American version. They were also more progressive, offering services, circles, training, and assessments online.

I enrolled in the SNUi's Platform Accreditation Scheme in January 2016, about three years after my journey began, and was able to do the extensive training and development via the internet. Once I passed the assessment in March 2018, which involved an interview with three assessors, a ten-minute inspirational address on Spiritualist philosophy, and two mediumship demonstrations within fifteen minutes, I moved on to the next level to do the training and assessment to become a certificate holder of the SNUi in speaking and demonstrating in March 2020, slightly more than seven years after I decided to become a medium. Yes, anyone can become a medium. It just took me a little longer than expected.

I decided not to pursue credentials in private sittings (readings), and I rarely do them anymore. Many clients come to a medium for answers, to seek advice from their loved ones in spirit, to apologize, to alleviate sorrow and guilt, and to know their loved ones are okay. In private sittings, the medium, in my experience, acts in some way as a grief counselor for those mourning the loss of their loved ones. While I do believe the spirit communicator can help address their loved one's grief, clients sometimes also need guidance from the medium herself. Private readings are a calling for those mediums who have the ability and training for this aspect of healing mediumship. Had I continued to do private sittings, I probably would have taken some classes in grief counseling.

My calling is for platform mediumship, where demonstrating that the soul survives is the primary purpose. A public demonstration of mediumship is sometimes a person's first encounter with a medium. Demonstrations are often low-cost or free. Healing occurs for everyone there because they are receiving evidence that our spirits survive, that physical death is not the end, that our loved ones are still with us, and they haven't fundamentally changed. Because it is a public platform, the spirit communicators often evoke laughter and tears of joy through their evidence, shared memories, and messages. It's a wonderous occasion to be reunited with those in spirit, and it's uplifting for all in the audience.

Of course, there are mediums who do both private sittings and demonstrations, and there is overlap in the type of healing each offers.

But what continues to amaze me is the intelligence of spirit in providing the right setting for the sitter's and communicator's needs.

Did I achieve my goal of having a two-way conversation with ancestors to aid my genealogical research? Yes and no. The communication wasn't like a phone conversation—I couldn't ask, "Hey! Where the heck are you in the 1860 census?" and have them respond by saying, "Look on page twenty-four. My name was misspelled." It happened in more subtle ways. When I researched and wrote Maria B. Hayden's biography, I know she helped me find her in unusual records that I doubt most researchers would have even known to look for. I talked to her constantly while writing her book. Then I remained open to random thoughts, hunches, and signs that might come from anywhere or anyone. One morning, I said to her, "This is it. We're at the end. If there's something else, speak now or forever hold your peace." That day, she roundaboutly led me to another source, one I'd unintentionally overlooked—followed by more obscure sources.

I do believe that most ancestors want to be found and remembered. They have a hand in our finding them and telling their stories. The ones who don't want to be found put roadblocks in our way. Genealogical research in and of itself is a communication.

But I discovered another way to get to know your ancestral spirits. See "A Genealogy Medium's Guide to Communicating with Your Ancestors" at the end of this book.

"I told my students my mother is a medium," Laurie said when she called one weekend.

Wait. What? Did I hear her correctly?

"Really? Did you make me out to sound like a kook?"

"No. I was teaching advanced bio, and we were exploring the limitations of science. We were talking about how science is the study of observable things or using tools to enhance our observation of observable things. I said there were some things that science can't test very well. One of those things is what happens when you die. There's no current, accurate scientific test for that."

I didn't say anything. I didn't want to spoil the moment.

She added, "Science, by its definition, is to be able to observe and measure things of the natural world. Some things fall into this supernatural category, and scientists don't think science can be done on those things. The test results aren't something we can recreate, and in science, you have to be able to recreate an experiment and get similar results. That's tricky to do with supernatural things. So that's why it came up. What are the limitations of science?"

Fair enough, although I knew there were scientists who'd tested mediums, and other scientists had recreated their experiment results.

"Then I told them my mom's a medium."

Could that have been just a wee hint of pride in her voice?

"Really? What was their reaction?"

"Some of them thought it was pretty cool. The skeptics stayed quiet."

And then Laurie had her own paranormal experience.

Her best friend since fourth grade, Shannon, had been admitted to the hospital. She had been diagnosed with stage four melanoma. Her body had become too weak for chemo.

Laurie drove to Washington state to see her and was upset because she'd heard that Shannon had asked that all treatment except painkillers be stopped. Shannon had accepted she was dying, but Laurie hadn't.

Laurie arrived in time to sit with Shannon, hold her hand, and reminisce with tears and laughter. She stayed with Shannon until midnight, then drove to Shannon's mother's house, where she stayed in the guest room.

Her voice grew somber when she told me about it over the phone. "I got to her mom's house about 12:30 and went to bed around one. I woke up and was on my left side, facing a wall with a bookcase. I felt like there was a presence in the room on the side I was facing. I turned away onto the other side that faced the window. It followed me and went to the other side, too." She paused. "And that was it."

"Did you open your eyes to see what it was?"

"No."

"Were you scared?"

"No."

"Did you feel like it was Shannon?"

"Yeah," Laurie said without hesitation.

"Did you feel like she touched you?"

"No. But I got the feeling somebody wanted my attention."

When Laurie woke around seven the next morning, she learned that Shannon had passed at 5:15 a.m. Shannon was one month shy of her thirty-third birthday.

Laurie and I talked about her experience again a few years later as I wrapped up this memoir.

"Where do you stand today on what happened?" I asked during a Zoom call. Laurie sat in her new science classroom on her lunch break. Since it was dress-down Friday, she wore a black school T-shirt with the words, *Be engaged. Be proud. Be together.* Instead of mad-scientist goggles around her neck, she wore a blue cloth facemask. The coronavirus pandemic hadn't left us yet.

"I think her condition was weighing pretty heavily on my mind that night, so I wasn't sleeping well. I think it was in my head."

She gave a nervous laugh, and I said, "That's fine." I wasn't going to try and tell her otherwise.

"My inclination," she continued, "was to believe that she was there because that's just easier to swallow. But the realist, the scientist in me, says that dreams are a result of what's been happening during the day. I think it was a dream. I think I was in and out of a light sleep."

Laurie was still a long way from accepting that there is life after death, although I am confident that, one day, she will believe it. After I'm gone, and she hears me rapping on the wall and my voice shouting in her ear, "I need water!" she'll be reminded of her pet hamster and how he banged his empty water bottle against his cage during the night. Then she'll know.

Still, a seismic shift gradually occurred between us over the years. We no longer felt the need to mark our territories, constantly retreating to our independent sides of the debate. I let go of my need to bombard her with my experiences and to convince her there is life after death. I respected her beliefs. And she respected mine.

"I think it's way cool that you're a medium," Laurie said on the Zoom call and smiled. She was nearly thirty-nine; her face radiated youth and beauty. She probably had a portrait in the closet that aged for her, or she had better Zoom filters than I did. "Of course, I have a hard time believing it," she said, "but, I don't know, it's a quirky thing to have in the family."

I laughed.

"If you're going to believe in something I don't believe in," she said, "at least it's a fun thing. I can get behind that."

Starting Your Own Journey

Everyone's journey into developing mediumship will be different. As you saw, mine meandered quite a bit, but I trusted the spirit world would take me down each path for a reason. Here are some of the lessons I teach my students.

Sitting in the Power Meditation

Not until I began studying with British mediums did I learn there is a specific meditation for developing mediumship. It's called "Sitting in the Power." There are many versions, and you can find some free ones on YouTube, but the basic premise is to build your own power, what some call raising your vibration, and connect your power with the Divine (God, the Source, the Universe, whatever your name is for that higher power).

Some instructors say you must sit for a given length of time for X number of days per week. I say, do what you can. If you can only do five minutes, something is better than nothing. If you can do it every day, great. If not, try for a few times a week. But if you can, make it a daily habit and sit for fifteen to twenty minutes at a time. Do it at a time when you won't fall asleep.

This is my version. Spend a couple minutes or longer on each step.

1. Sit comfortably in a chair with your feet flat on the ground.
2. Close your eyes and take several deep breaths. Now move your awareness to your heart, and imagine you are breathing in and out through your heart.
3. Fill your heart with gratitude for someone, something, or some place. That gratitude in your heart is your power and light.
4. Now imagine you are expanding that gratitude or light outward so it fills the room you sit in.
5. Then imagine there is a bright white light above you (this is the God of your understanding), and your power and light are moving toward it and blending with it.
6. As you sit in the power of this light, ask that it give you as much power and light as your soul can absorb at this point in your journey. Sit in this power and light for as long as you like.
7. Now invite your team of spirit guides to join you in that Divine power and light. Ask them to blend with you, to attune to you and you to them. Trust this is happening whether you feel anything or not. Sit with them for however long you like.
8. Ask them to assist and guide you in your journey. Or ask for whatever guidance you need in that moment. But don't expect immediate answers! Answers may come several days later and in unexpected ways. Be open to anything that comes your way.
9. Thank your spirit team and the God of your understanding.
10. Slowly return to your body by wiggling your toes and fingers and stretching.

Does Your Mediumship Have Heart?

Point to yourself. Yes, point to yourself. Where did you point? Remember where you pointed as you read on.

When we pass into spirit, our memories, emotions, and personality live on. How do we communicate with these immaterial and immortal characteristics? We often say it's through telepathy (mind-to-mind) or a soul-to-soul connection. But I suggest it might be more through a heart-to-heart connection.

Some mediumship instructors teach connecting with spirit through the solar plexus. They say that this is the so-called center of being and therefore the seat of the soul. Yet "almost every spiritual tradition and all the major world religions talk about the heart being the access point to the soul," says Rollin McCraty, PhD, in *The Power of the Heart*. "And the research is really starting to show that they've been right all along."

Okay. Where did you point when you pointed to yourself? Was it to your heart? If so, there's a reason for that.

If you examine any illustration of the seven chakras, or energy centers, the heart is at the center. It connects our physical biology (the lower three chakras) with our psychological and spiritual energy (the upper three chakras). Likewise, according to medical intuitive Carolyn Myss, PhD, author of *Anatomy of the Spirit: The Seven Stages of Power and Healing*, all illnesses and diseases typically originate in one of the lower three chakras, of which the solar plexus is part, and then the illness or disease manifests there or elsewhere in the body. So, if the solar plexus connects us to our physical biology and can be the root of disease, it doesn't make sense to work mediumistically from that energy center. It makes more sense to work from the heart, the energetic center, the root of emotion, intuition, and clairsentience.

Studies through the HeartMath Institute show that we receive external information through the heart first. Founded in 1991, "HeartMath developed a system of effective, scientifically based tools and technologies to bridge the intuitive connection between heart and mind and deepen our connection with the hearts of others." Researchers discovered this by hooking up volunteers to a variety of sensors to measure brain waves, heartbeats, and more, then showing the participants pleasant and unpleasant images on a computer screen. "When we analyzed all the data, the results were astounding. The heart seemed to know the images before the participants ever saw the images with their eyes. . . . A lot of people say that I don't feel at my heart. I feel it in the gut. But here's what's really happening. The information comes to the heart first." Then the researchers noted a brain response, followed by a bodily response, or gut feeling.

According to the HeartMath researchers in "The Heart-Brain Connection," "It is not as commonly known that *the heart actually sends more signals to the brain than the brain sends to the heart!* Moreover, these heart signals have a significant effect on brain function—influencing emotional processing as well as higher cognitive faculties such as attention, perception, memory, and problem-solving. In other words, not only does the heart respond to the brain, but the brain continuously responds to the heart."

According to *Science of the Heart: Exploring the Role of the Heart in Human Performance*, HeartMath researchers also found that "the heart is the most powerful source of electromagnetic energy in the human body, producing the largest rhythmic electromagnetic field of any of the body's organs. The heart's electrical field is about 60 times greater in amplitude than the electrical activity generated by the brain." This field, which permeates every cell of the body and envelops the entire physical body, can be measured with magnetometers as far away as *eight to ten feet* from the body, says *The HeartMath Solution* by Doc Childre and Howard Martin with Donna Beech. After physical death, this energy field, or aura or spirit body, if you like, increases even more in frequency and vibration once freed from the physical body.

Researchers refer to this as the "intuitive heart" or "energetic heart." Like the mind, which can survive and exist without a physical brain, the intuitive, energetic heart can survive without a physical heart.

The HeartMath's scientific studies have also found that the intuitive, energetic heart is an access point to our higher self, which can help us communicate at a higher level with the higher self and, it follows, with the spirit world. The energetic heart contains our history, our memories, our personalities. The mind and heart are synergistic, and these energetic sources make up the foundation of our thoughts and emotions. The intuitive, energetic heart is what many people associate with the "inner voice." This heart intelligence also enables us to communicate with each other on an unseen energetic level, whether in the body or not.

Thus, the science shows that it makes perfect sense to focus our awareness on our hearts when developing mediumship and communicating with spirit, rather than on the solar plexus. It takes just a couple of moments to make that connection. Close your eyes, take three deep breaths, and then shift your awareness to the center of your chest, to your heart. Imagine you are breathing in and out through your heart. Fill your heart with a positive emotion: appreciation or gratitude for someone, something, or some place. Then consciously expand that feeling beyond and all around you. As you expand your energy, set the intention to connect with a spirit communicator. It's best to feel their energy coming from behind you, however, so you don't unintentionally link psychically with the sitter (recipient).

As the HeartMath research has shown, information is detected first by the heart, so it follows that we would perceive spirit first through the heart (clairsentience); then we get a picture (clairvoyance) or sounds (clairaudience), then a "clairknowing" in our gut. Although we might be cognizant of the picture first, or the gut feeling, the emotion or story that goes with that picture or gut reaction has already been communicated through the heart. By returning our awareness to the heart, we can discover the meaning behind the picture or gut reaction that spirit wants to communicate.

When doing a private sitting or demonstration, if you feel like the information has gone dry or you've lost the connection, bring your awareness back to your heart, breathe through the heart, expand, and reconnect with the communicator. There is no need to ask spirit to come closer. Spirit knows where they are supposed to be. *You* need to make the additional effort to move your energetic heart into their vibrational field.

Now point to yourself again. Did you point to your heart? If so, give this heart method of communicating with spirit a try. You might find it makes a big difference in developing your mediumship.

Mediumship Problem-Solving

Having now taught mediumship development for several years, I've realized that making a connection to the spirit world is actually the easy part. Problem-solving in the moment is the difficult part. That means you know what to do when you get a "no" to information you've given. Confidence in problem-solving is how you develop trust and confidence in your mediumship. There can be many reasons a medium will get a "no," but I've found the primary reason is the medium's misinterpretation of what the spirit person is trying to say. When I ask students to tell me exactly what they received and how they received it, they invariably restate the information in a different way, and then they get a "yes." Just give what you get.

Training in the so-called British method means the spirit person is not using symbols but is pretty straightforward. The message, which is often based on the evidence, may be symbolic, but the identifying information itself will be concrete. For example, when spirit shows a rose, it can be any number of things: the name Rose, the spirit liked roses, the spirit grew roses, the spirit was allergic to roses. How will you know? You ask! When you see a rose, ask the spirit communicator, "What do you want me to say about the rose?" Then feel through your clairsentience for the answer. That's the only way to know what the spirit is trying to communicate.

But be careful how you phrase your questions. You don't want your own mind to fill in the answers. It's best to be general, and simply ask, "What do you want me to say next?" Then bring your awareness back to your heart, the seat of your clairsentience. Trust, too, that the spirit person knows exactly what information to give you to pass along to the recipient so their loved one will be recognized.

Of course, there are other reasons you might get a "no": you're with the wrong recipient, you've overstated or understated something, you've given the wrong relationship, the information is about the recipient and not the communicator, the recipient is trying to make the information fit to someone else they have in mind, or the recipient just doesn't remember what the spirit remembers. With experience, all these possibilities will become second nature, and you will be able to problem-solve why the recipient gave you a "no."

A Genealogy Medium's Guide to Communicating with Your Ancestors

Remember, the simple act of researching ancestors opens the door to communication. Most ancestors want to be found and are aware of the work you are doing. You just need to become aware of the clues and responses they are giving you. You can certainly ask them questions mentally or aloud, but the answers often won't come back to you in a direct form. The answer can come in many different ways: a hunch or a feeling, in something you read, or something you see or hear on TV or in conversation.

One method of communication that works well is called *psychometry*, the reading of an object's energy. The famous English medium Gordon Higginson, in his memoir *On the Side of Angels*, said that his mother trained him as a psychometrist. He wrote, "Psychometry is the history, the thoughts, feelings, and ambitions of the person who had handled the article." The science of physics tells us that everything is made up of energy, and energy vibrates at various rates. The theory behind psychometry is that objects absorb and retain the energy or vibrations of the owner, which a psychometrist can then read. But how psychometrists receive the impressions from the vibration is open for debate.

One school of thought is the medium is sensitive to the energy vibrations, which she then "reads" as impressions through clairsentience and her other clairs. Another theory is the energy of the object is of a spirit nature, and the object is imprinted with the spirit-self of the owner, and this is what the medium senses. A third possibility is the object becomes the conduit between the medium and the spirit of the owner, which in turn leads to communication coming from the spirit person.

The word *psychometry* comes from the Greek *psyche* ("soul") and *metron* ("measure"), which literally means "soul measuring." Joseph R. Buchanan, MD (1814–1899), an American physician and professor of physiology at the Eclectic Medical Institute in Covington, Kentucky, coined the term in his 1842 book, *Manual of Psychometry: The Dawn of a New Civilization*. (Buchanan's book is some five hundred pages and not light reading. Instead, you may want to try the more compact book, Ted Andrews's *How to Do Psychic Readings through Touch*.) Buchanan posits that the essential nature of the psychometric faculty is intuition, but that "feeling, hearing, seeing and sympathetic impression will act in unison to give the delicate and profound knowledge."

You can perform psychometry on objects owned or worn only by your ancestor, on photographs of the person, and on a person's handwriting. Typically, you would hold the item, image, or handwriting between your hands, and feel the information it tells you. In other words, trust the impressions and thoughts that pop into your mind and write them down. If using a photograph, make sure the ancestor is the only one in the image. The same with handwriting. If there is more than one person's handwriting on a document, you could pick up on the other person's energy. Scan and isolate the person's image or handwriting. You do not need to use the original. Then place the handwriting between your hands and focus on what you feel. With practice, your accuracy will increase, and you will be able to pick up the energy of the person.

I trained myself in psychometry by having Jim print out pictures of his relatives and ancestors or of famous people; then he would put one each in a manila envelope. Each morning, I would hold one envelope between my hands and at heart level and call out my impressions and thoughts—about the person's gender, education, occupation, hobbies and interests, personality, time period the person lived during, etc. Jim would write down what I said. My goal was twenty pieces of information per enveloped image. Then Jim would open the envelope to see whose photo it was and tell me how accurate I was.

We then moved on to pieces of writing. It could be an email, a handwritten letter, or something published. It didn't matter. The writer's energy is imprinted in the writer's words. As with photographs, he put each one in a manila envelope. We went through the same process of giving twenty pieces of information per writing or envelope.

With practice, my psychometry readings were typically 80 percent accurate.

I once did a private sitting for a friend who wanted to link with his grandmother. She had passed into spirit when he was three, and he was hoping to learn the true identity of her mother, as she was raised by someone else in the family. I wasn't optimistic that I could get specific information like that. I informed him, too, that I couldn't guarantee I would even be able to connect with her. Spirit people do not appear on command. When I did the reading, it seemed as if everyone else he knew in spirit stepped forward except his grandmother.

He wore on his pinkie finger his grandmother's engagement ring, so I offered to perform psychometry on it. But I let him know that I might also pick up on his energy as he had been wearing the ring for a few years.

I clasped the ring between the palms of my hands and set the intent to feel only her energy and to receive information through clairsentience. The energy of the ring told an emotional story of abuse and also one of sadness over the loss of a child. Unfortunately, the recipient did not know whether that was the case with his grandmother. At one point, I felt the grandmother was with me in spirit, and she impressed upon me to put the ring down, so I did. Then she communicated to me that she was emotionally abandoned by her mother and that her mother had some kind of mental illness. Again, unfortunately, the recipient could not confirm the information I received from her. He would have to do more research to validate it.

Several days after I did the reading, he sent me a photograph of his grandmother as a child. She was an adorable little girl of about five, her dark hair curled in ringlets with a big bow affixed. She held her doll for the photograph. What my friend hadn't noticed about the photograph, however, which I did, was not only a defiant look in her eyes and that her hands were clenched, but also the remnant discoloration of a black eye.

I asked another medium to connect with the photograph and did not tell her anything about what I had received. She said she felt "there was a strong vibe of tension in the family."

While you probably won't get specific names and dates doing psychometry, you can get a feel for an ancestor's personality and life story. Some information you'll be able to validate through your research or through talking with relatives. But, if possible, have another sensitive person or medium who knows nothing about the person do psychometry to corroborate your impressions.

And, of course, you can engage a medium to see if he or she can connect with your ancestor. I recommend you look for one who holds a certificate or diploma from the Spiritualists' National Union. You will know that they have been well trained and have passed rigorous assessments. To find an award holder, go to https://www.snu.org.uk/Pages/Category/award-holders, or contact a national representative here: https://snui.org.uk/national-representatives.

Do keep your expectations in check: spirits do not respond on demand, and depending on the medium's abilities, he or she may not be able to receive specific details such as names, dates, and places. Additionally, some of our more distant ancestors may have ascended on the other side to a higher plane of vibration, which the medium's vibration is unable to reach. The spirit must lower his or her vibration to get to the medium's level, while the medium has to raise hers. This is why you are more likely to hear from the generations of your parents, grandparents, and perhaps great-grandparents, and not much further back. Still, it's always worth a try. The spirit world never ceases to amaze me.

Finding a Teacher and Suggested Reading

There are many mediums who teach mediumship. I recommend one who either teaches at the Arthur Findlay College in Stansted, England, was trained there, or who has studied with one of their tutors. Many now come to America to do workshops, or they teach online. Some also teach online for the Spiritualists' National Union International: https://snui.org.uk. The other thing to look for in a teacher is one whose method and practice of teaching feels right to you. If it doesn't resonate with you, look for another teacher.

While it's natural to sample several teachers when you start your journey, at some point, pick one or two and stick with them. You don't want to be confused when one teacher says to do it this way and another says to do it that way. You also don't want to confuse your spirit team. They need to know how you want to work. Your consistency is part of the key to successful mediumship.

What you don't want in a teacher is someone who teaches fear of the spirit world, that you have to do certain rituals, such as light candles, smudge, protect yourself, open and close chakras, and so forth. Communicating with people in the spirit world is as natural as communicating with your next-door neighbor. Yes, there are people here in the physical world you wouldn't choose to hang out with. But if we accept that like attracts like, then you won't attract those individuals from the spirit world.

While there are many books on developing mediumship on the market, I really recommend just one: *Paul, Man of Spirit: The World of Paul Jacobs* by Jenni Gomes. It is part biography, but it is also a development guide. Most everything Paul teaches in his workshops is contained in that book. Of course, if you can do a workshop with Paul, either in person or online, I doubt you'll be disappointed. He has a no-nonsense and logical approach to his teaching of mediumship. He is a natural-born teacher, and truly cares about all of his students and their mediumship development and advancement. His website is https://www.mediumpauljacobs.com/.

To learn more about Spiritualism and the spirit world, I recommend *The Philosophy of Spiritualism* by Barry Oates, David Hopkins, and Carole Austen, and any books in the Silver Birch series. Just enter "Silver Birch" in Amazon's book search.

Although not written by a Spiritualist, *Testimony of Light: An Extraordinary Message of Life After Death* by Helen Greaves, who received spirit communication from her friend Frances Banks, an Anglican nun, offers one of the best descriptions of the spirit world that I've read.

Finally, look for Vi Kipling's *Myths and Misconceptions of Spiritualism*. Unfortunately, the only place it may be available is through the Arthur Findlay College Bookshop, https://www.snu.org.uk/shop/myths-and-misconceptions-of-spiritualism-vi-kipling-fsnu. But it's well worth reading to dispel many of the common myths, not just about Spiritualism but about mediumship in general.

Enjoy your journey!

Acknowledgments

Everyone along my journey was instrumental in my development as a medium—teachers, friends, students, clients, colleagues, authors, skeptics, and acquaintances. I couldn't include them all in my story, otherwise this book would be a ten-pound tome! And if I named them all here, the acknowledgments would be longer than this book. But each contributed to the medium I am today.

Joseph Ditta and Sue Repko graciously read and provided helpful feedback on a draft of this manuscript.

Everyone at Köehler Books has been wonderful to work with from John Koehler, president and publisher; to Joe Coccaro, vice president and executive editor, who recommended acquiring my book for traditional publishing; to Danielle Koehler, who did a fantastic job designing my new website, TheGenealogyMedium.com, and the cover for this book; and to Miranda Dillon, for her eagle eye as my editor.

My daughter, Laurie, has come to accept that her mom is not only a medium but a writer, too, which means her life often gets portrayed in print. I'm grateful she doesn't mind.

Of course, my biggest supporter and fan is my partner, Jim Warren. He reads everything I write and offers suggestions—some I take, some I don't—but I'm always appreciative of his feedback. Jim is my spirit guide in the physical world, and for that, I'm truly blessed.

Other books by Sharon DeBartolo Carmack

Researching Ancestors in Irish Records

If We Can Winter This: Essays and Genealogies, The Gordon Family of County Leitrim, Ireland, and The Norris Family of County Tyrone, (now) Northern Ireland

In Search of Maria B. Hayden: The American Medium Who Brought Spiritualism to the U.K.

Inheriting the Gordon Hips

The Elements of Genealogical Style: A Simplified Style and Citation Manual for Writers of Genealogies and Family Histories

Tell It Short: A Guide to Writing Your Family History in Brief

With Two Potatoes in His Pocket: The History of the McNamara and McGuire Families of Ireland and Richmond, Virginia

The History of the Ferry, Sferra, Jeney, Hillman, and Hopkins Families

The Family History of Daniel Donovan and Catherine Caughlin, co-authored with James W. Warren

The Riggs Family of Accomack County, Virginia, and Louisiana, ca. 1687 to 1943

Carmack's Guide to Copyright & Contracts: A Primer for Genealogists, Writers & Researchers

The Family Tree Guide to Finding Your Ellis Island Ancestors

Italians in Transition: The Vallarelli Family of Terlizzi, Italy, and Westchester County, New York and The DeBartolo Family of Terlizzi, Italy, New York, and San Francisco, California

You Can Write Your Family History

A Sense of Duty: The Life and Times of Jay Roscoe Rhoads and his wife, Mary Grace Rudolph

Your Guide to Cemetery Research

My Wild Irish Rose: The Life of Rose (Norris) (O'Connor) Fitzhugh and her mother Delia (Gordon) Norris

David and Charlotte Hawes (Buckner) Stuart of King George County, Virginia, Including Three Generations of Their Descendants

A Genealogist's Guide to Discovering Your Immigrant and Ethnic Ancestors

American Lives and Lines, co-authored with Roger D. Joslyn

Organizing Your Family History Search

A Genealogist's Guide to Discovering Your Female Ancestors

Italian-American Family History: A Guide to Researching and Writing About Your Heritage

The Genealogy Sourcebook

Communities at Rest: An Inventory and Field Study of Five Eastern Colorado Cemeteries

The Ebetino and Vallarelli Family History: Italian Immigrants to Westchester County, New York

About the Author

Sharon DeBartolo Carmack is a Certified Genealogist® with an MFA in creative nonfiction writing. She received a certificate in demonstrating mediumship and an advanced academic diploma from the Spiritualists' National Union in the UK. Sharon is the author of twenty-six books, including the best-selling guides *Organizing Your Family History Search; A Genealogist's Guide to Discovering Your Female Ancestors; Your Guide to Cemetery Research; You Can Write Your Family History; Tell It Short: A Guide to Writing Your Family History in Brief;* and the recent biography, *In Search of Maria B. Hayden: The American Medium Who Brought Spiritualism to the U.K.* Her work has appeared in almost every major genealogical journal, as well as *Brevity, Creative Nonfiction, Portland Review, Hippocampus Magazine, Phoebe: A Journal of Literature and Art, Steinbeck Review,* and *Literary Hub,* to name a few. She is part of the English adjunct faculty for Southern New Hampshire University and the genealogy adjunct faculty for Salt Lake Community College. Sharon can be reached through her websites, www.TheGenealogyMedium.com and www.SharonCarmack.com.

CPSIA information can be obtained
at www.ICGtesting.com
Printed in the USA
BVHW070324040622
638839BV00003B/17